Writing with POWER

Language Skills Practice
Grammar, Usage, and Mechanics

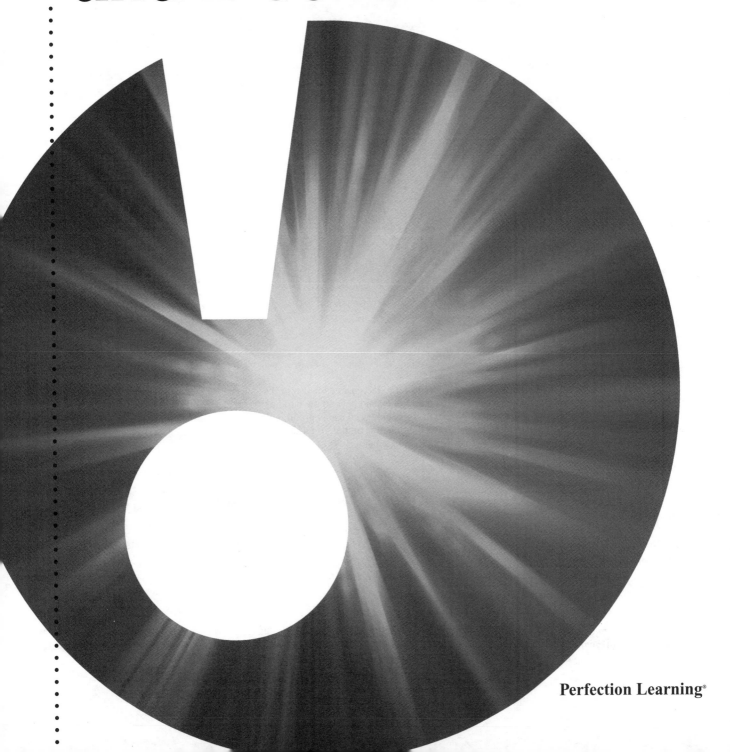

Perfection Learning®

Printed in the United States of America.

18 19 20 21 22   PP   24 23 22 21 20

For information, contact
Perfection Learning® Corporation
1000 North Second Avenue, P.O. Box 500
Logan, Iowa 51546-0500
Phone: 1-800-831-4190 • Fax: 1-800-543-2745
perfectionlearning.com

77953
ISBN-13: 978-0-7891-7976-0
ISBN-10: 0-7891-7976-8

Table of Contents

continued

Table of Contents *continued*

CHAPTER 12 Determining Nouns

[12A] A **noun** is the name of a person, place, thing, or idea.

> **EXERCISE** Underline each word that is used as a noun in the following sentences.

1. A wolf howled at the moon through the trees.

2. The shark swallowed a bluefish in one swift movement.

3. My sister is setting the table with Mom's finest china.

4. The necklace could not be found on the dresser or the countertop.

5. Lightning ignited a fire in the hayloft and destroyed the barn.

6. That dog with the dark spots is a spaniel.

7. Your papers and old-fashioned manual typewriter have been moved to the living room.

8. Her brother-in-law was the head lifeguard at the lake.

9. The airplane made stops in three countries.

10. In football a touchdown is worth more points than a field goal.

11. During the summers Rose Park needs lifeguards for its pool.

12. Whenever I smell pizza, my mouth starts to water.

13. El Dorado is a legendary city of gold hidden in the Amazon Basin.

14. The animated films of Japanese director Hayao Miyazaki are beloved around the world.

15. There are around 40,000 species of spiders, but all have eight legs and make webs.

CHAPTER 12 Common and Proper Nouns

[12A.2] A **common noun** names any person, place, or thing. A **proper noun** names a particular person, place, or thing.

> **EXERCISE** Write C if the underlined word or group of words is a common noun or P if it is a proper noun.

_____ 1. Many jobs and apartment rentals are listed in the classifieds section of <u>The New York Times</u>.

_____ 2. Dr. Chang is looking for a new <u>nurse</u> to join his surgical team at the hospital.

_____ 3. A waiter, busboy, and <u>dishwasher</u> are needed at the Fish Pot.

_____ 4. Another <u>restaurant</u> on Main Street needs a dishwasher and busboy also.

_____ 5. <u>Bailey Products</u> is looking for drivers to deliver its packages across town.

_____ 6. A store on Center Avenue wants a <u>cashier</u> on a full-time basis.

_____ 7. Painters are needed this weekend for work on the <u>Harvard Bridge</u>.

_____ 8. <u>Wolpert Hardware</u> needs a clerk to handle inventory in the lawnmower section.

_____ 9. The Ace Health Club needs two workers to clean the pool and <u>sauna</u>.

_____ 10. The <u>Pittsburgh Pirates</u> will be playing in a new stadium soon.

_____ 11. I read Kafka's <u>The Trial</u> when I was on the school bus.

_____ 12. The <u>park</u> is a safe place to jog in the evening.

_____ 13. My father grew up in <u>Lubbock</u>, Texas.

_____ 14. I never listened to the musical group before my older brother bought their <u>CD</u>.

_____ 15. <u>President Johnson</u> was from Texas.

CHAPTER 12 Identifying Proper, Compound, and Collective Nouns

[12A.3] A noun that includes more than one word is called a **compound noun**.

[12A.4] A **collective noun** names a group of people or things.

EXERCISE A Decide whether the underlined word in each sentence is a proper noun, a compound noun, or a collective noun.

_____ 1. My <u>sister-in-law</u> just bought a new pair of dungarees.
   A proper noun
   B compound noun
   C collective noun

_____ 2. Originally the word referred to a heavy cotton from <u>Dhungaree</u>, which is in India.
   A proper noun
   B compound noun
   C collective noun

_____ 3. The <u>butterfly</u> flew from flower to flower in our front garden.
   A proper noun
   B compound noun
   C collective noun

_____ 4. A sweater called a jersey was first worn by fishers on <u>Jersey</u>, an island off the coast of England.
   A proper noun
   B compound noun
   C collective noun

_____ 5. Today football <u>teams</u> wear jerseys as part of their uniforms.
   A proper noun
   B compound noun
   C collective noun

EXERCISE B Underline all of the proper, compound, and collective nouns in the following sentences. Write the kind of noun above each one.

6. Some clothes are named for a member of a famous family.

7. A special kind of coat was often worn by an English lord whose name was Raglan.

8. An overcoat with large sleeves and shoulders became known as a raglan.

9. When traveling to England, it is wise to take a raincoat.

10. If you are in a dance troupe or enjoy exercise, you have probably worn a leotard.

11. You owe the development of this comfortable outfit to a performer on the trapeze.

12. The Prime Minister will address the nation later today.

CHAPTER 12 Pronoun Antecedents

[12B] A **pronoun** is a word that takes the place of one or more nouns.

[12B.1] The noun a pronoun refers to or replaces is called its **antecedent**.

EXERCISE Circle the antecedent for each underlined pronoun.

1. Ellen carried <u>her</u> umbrella to school.

2. Walter said, "<u>I</u> like mashed potatoes best."

3. Steve asked Anita to go to the dance with <u>him</u>.

4. Randy and Margo said <u>they</u> were going to the movies.

5. Sandy told Robert that <u>she</u> was having a party.

6. The sky has a rosy tint to <u>it</u>.

7. Did Clara and Ann wear <u>their</u> uniforms?

8. Jeff asked Leda, "Are <u>you</u> leaving now?"

9. Albert said that <u>he</u> was going to play hockey.

10. The coach asked the team, "Are <u>you</u> ready to win?"

11. This bridge has several loose planks in <u>it</u>.

12. Jill asked the customer, "May I help <u>you</u>?"

13. When will this tree lose <u>its</u> leaves for the winter?

14. Tanya said to Katarina, "<u>I</u>'m ready for summer break!"

15. The people in the audience clapped <u>their</u> hands enthusiastically.

Name **Date**

CHAPTER 12 — Personal Pronouns

EXERCISE A Underline the personal pronoun(s) in each sentence. Then draw an arrow to the antecedent(s) of the underlined pronoun.

1. The 1984 Boston Marathon was on its way.

2. There was a light rain, and it cooled the runners as they ran.

3. "We think Lorraine Moller will be our winner," said several women.

4. Lorraine Moller was from New Zealand, and she had two goals in the marathon.

5. Moller wanted to win and to make her country's Olympic team as well.

6. "You can win!" some enthusiastic onlookers shouted to Moller.

7. Other people handed Moller water and towels as she ran past them.

8. Moller did win the marathon that year, and she went on to place fifth in the Olympic marathon.

EXERCISE B Rewrite each sentence, replacing unnecessary nouns with pronouns.

9. Katie forgot Katie's lunch again.

10. The batter dropped the bat on the batter's toe.

11. Elaine did not recognize the man behind the mask, but the man knew Elaine.

12. Julie missed Rafael and sent Rafael fourteen postcards from Paris.

13. The dog was still scratching the dog's ear.

14. "Don't forget to write to Sam this summer," Sam urged.

CHAPTER 12 — Other Kinds of Pronouns

[12B.2] **Reflexive pronouns** and **intensive pronouns** refer to or emphasize another noun or pronoun.

[12B.3] **Indefinite pronouns** refer to unnamed people, places, things, or ideas.

[12B.4] **Demonstrative pronouns** point out a specific person, place, thing, or idea.

[12B.5] **Interrogative pronouns** are used to ask questions.

EXERCISE Label each underlined pronoun as personal, reflexive, indefinite, demonstrative, interrogative, or intensive.

---

(1) Anyone eating a lot of cereal should take an interest in the box as well as in **(2)** its contents. By following the instructions on the box, **(3)** you **(4)** yourself may be the happy recipient of such welcome items as **(5)** these: insulated mugs, personalized pens, recipe boxes, digital watches, and exercise mats. **(6)** Who could resist such delightful gifts? All **(7)** you need do is send in **(8)** something like a coupon—and perhaps some money.

Years ago almost **(9)** everyone collected cereal box tops. **(10)** What did people receive in those days? The gifts were significantly different from **(11)** those offered today. In the old days, **(12)** they were usually connected with movie stars or radio show heroes. The gifts weren't useful. Instead, the main purpose of **(13)** them was to allow **(14)** anyone to become a member of **(15)** something—a club, for instance. Fans of radio cowboy Tom Mix used the rings **(16)** they received to identify **(17)** themselves as Tom Mix fans. Captain Marvel club members used the decoders **(18)** they **(19)** themselves received to save friends, family members, and others in danger. **(20)** Those were indeed items to be treasured.

---

1. _____
2. _____
3. _____
4. _____
5. _____
6. _____
7. _____
8. _____
9. _____
10. _____

11. _____
12. _____
13. _____
14. _____
15. _____
16. _____
17. _____
18. _____
19. _____
20. _____

CHAPTER 12   Nouns and Pronouns Review

EXERCISE Identify each underlined word or group of words in the paragraph below.

In the 1970s, **(1)** magician James Randi warned paranormal researchers that **(2)** they were being fooled. **(3)** Anyone could appear to be psychic by using simple tricks. To prove his point, **(4)** Randi sent two young magicians to Washington University to pose as psychics. The **(5)** duo pretended not to know each other but worked together to deceive the researchers. Randi instructed them to reveal **(6)** themselves as fakes if they were asked how they did it, but they were never asked. The young men grew famous doing **(7)** this, and when Randi told the researchers about the **(8)** setup, there were some who insisted the men were not fakes. **(9)** Who would have guessed that scientists would put their **(10)** faith in psychics?

_____ 1. **A** abstract noun
B common noun
C proper noun
D collective noun

_____ 2. **A** personal pronoun
B demonstrative pronoun
C reflexive pronoun
D indefinite pronoun

_____ 3. **A** personal pronoun
B demonstrative pronoun
C reflexive pronoun
D indefinite pronoun

_____ 4. **A** common noun
B abstract noun
C proper noun
D compound noun

_____ 5. **A** collective noun
B abstract noun
C proper noun
D compound noun

_____ 6. **A** interrogative pronoun
B personal pronoun
C demonstrative pronoun
D reflexive pronoun

_____ 7. **A** interrogative pronoun
B intensive pronoun
C demonstrative pronoun
D reflexive pronoun

_____ 8. **A** proper noun
B concrete noun
C compound noun
D collective noun

_____ 9. **A** demonstrative pronoun
B reflexive pronoun
C reciprocal pronoun
D interrogative pronoun

_____ 10. **A** proper noun
B abstract noun
C concrete noun
D collective noun

CHAPTER 13 Action Verbs

[13A] A **verb** is a word that expresses action or a state of being.
[13A.1] An **actionverb** tells what action a subject is performing.

EXERCISE Underline the action verb in each sentence.

1. Cara apologized for her neglect.

2. We compared the prices of the ties.

3. The strong quarterback completed the pass.

4. I need four books for my report on early computers.

5. The diver won a medal.

6. A vase of roses sits on the piano.

7. A bright red convertible passed us on the highway.

8. Chantelle outlined her report carefully.

9. We worried about rain all day.

10. All of the guests arrived on time.

11. The surgeon operates twice daily.

12. The giraffe and the deer stared at each other.

13. They said good-bye tearfully.

14. Han pitched a no-hitter yesterday afternoon.

15. Mrs. Oren owns the bookshop.

16. The cat likes its catnip mouse.

17. The entire team missed the bus to Atlanta.

18. Everyone in the room applauded.

CHAPTER 13 Verb Phrases

[13A.2] A **verbphrase** includes a main verb plus any helping, or auxiliary, verbs.

EXERCISE Select the verb phrase for each sentence.

_____ 1. Most small bears can climb trees.

    A bears
    B climb
    C can climb
    D trees

_____ 2. My grandparents will be visiting us for two weeks.

    A will be visiting
    B two weeks
    C grandparents
    D be visiting

_____ 3. The telephone has been ringing all day.

    A ringing
    B all day
    C telephone
    D has been ringing

_____ 4. Water is always dripping in the sink.

    A always dripping
    B in the sink
    C is dripping
    D water

_____ 5. Jamie is wearing her favorite shirt today.

    A Jamie
    B is wearing
    C favorite
    D today

_____ 6. We have lived in Florida for six years.

    A have lived
    B lived
    C in Florida
    D years

_____ 7. You should always exercise in comfortable shoes.

    A should always
    B in shoes
    C should exercise
    D you

_____ 8. People were training dogs in prehistoric times.

    A were training
    B in times
    C people
    D training

_____ 9. My favorite candidate was elected student council president.

    A my favorite
    B candidate
    C was
    D was elected

_____ 10. The American Youth Hostels organization was founded in 1934.

    A was
    B founded
    C was founded
    D was founded in 1934

_____ 11. The movement had begun in Germany in 1909.

    A had
    B begun
    C had begun
    D had begun in Germany

_____ 12. Richard Shirrman would take his students on nature hikes.

    A would take his students
    B would take
    C take
    D would

_____ 13. Germany did not have many accommodations for them.

    A did have
    B did not have
    C have accommodations
    D have many accommodations

Name _____ Date _____

CHAPTER 13 **Verb Phrases**

EXERCISE Underline the verb phrase in each sentence.

(1) People are stung by bees, wasps, and hornets every summer. (2) The venom can cause death

in certain people. (3) Thousands of people have died from insect stings. (4) Injections of venom can

help allergic people. (5) It must be given carefully in small doses. (6) Once scientists could not obtain

venom from insects easily. (7) They have now found a way. (8) A cold insect will usually fall into

a light sleep. (9) It can be awakened suddenly. (10) A spurt of venom will be released by the angry

insect. (11) Several hundred insects can be "milked" this way every day. (12) This new source of

venom has saved many lives.

CHAPTER 13   Transitive Verbs and Intransitive Verbs

[13B.1] A **transitiveverb** is an action verb that passes the action from a doer to a receiver. An **intransitiveverb** expresses action or states something about the subject but does not pass the action from a doer to a receiver.

EXERCISEA   Write T in the blank if the underlined verb is transitive and I if the verb is intransitive.

_____   1. Ellyse schooled the young horse for the show.

_____   2. The eagle soared in the sky.

_____   3. They drove the truck across the high bridge.

_____   4. Quickly Audrey collected her papers.

_____   5. We dashed into the doorway because of the storm.

_____   6. The space shuttle landed at noon.

_____   7. The enthusiastic audience applauded the candidates.

_____   8. Sometimes you can distinguish a meteorite from an ordinary rock by its weight.

_____   9. Suddenly lightning struck the massive tree.

EXERCISEB   Underline the action verb in each sentence. Then label it T for transitive or I for intransitive in the blank provided.

_____   10. Eagles keep the same nests throughout their lives.

_____   11. Hummingbirds sometimes fly backwards.

_____   12. The dog buried its bone in the backyard.

_____   13. The family eats fresh vegetables every day.

_____   14. An orange moon hung in the evening sky.

_____   15. Strawberries contain more vitamin C than oranges.

_____   16. The Empire State Building has 6,400 windows.

CHAPTER 13   Linking Verbs

EXERCISE A   Choose the correct linking verb and the two words that the verb links.

_____ 1. John's computer is the new, red one.
    A is: John's, new
    B is: computer, one
    C one: computer, new
    D one: new, red

_____ 2. The weather in Florida has been terrible.
    A weather: Florida, terrible
    B has: weather, been
    C has been: Florida, terrible
    D has been: weather, terrible

_____ 3. According to the weatherman, tomorrow should be better.
    A should be: tomorrow, better
    B should be: weatherman, better
    C weatherman: tomorrow, better
    D weatherman: should, better

_____ 4. My favorite uncle should have been a clown.
    A should have been: favorite, clown
    B should have been: uncle, clown
    C been: favorite, clown
    D been: uncle, clown

_____ 5. That strange, furry fruit may be a kiwi.
    A may: furry, fruit
    B may: fruit, kiwi
    C may be: fruit, kiwi
    D may be: strange, furry

EXERCISE B   Underline the linking verbs in the following sentences. Than circle the two words the verb links.

6. The party should have been over by 10:30.

7. The Chinese dinner smelled absolutely delicious.

8. Emily is a waitress at the Lobster Pit Restaurant.

9. She grew nervous before the audition but became calm during her song.

10. Some vegetables taste awful to little children.

11. That mechanical tiger looks, feels, and sounds real.

12. The weather has not turned cold yet.

CHAPTER 13 Distinguishing Between Linking Verbs and Action Verbs

[13A.1] An **actionverb** tells what action a subject is performing.

[13C] A **linkingverb** links the subject with another word in the sentence. The other word either renames or describes the subject.

EXERCISEA Decide whether the underlined word(s) is a linking or an action verb.

_____ 1. Rhonda's arm <u>felt</u> itchy from the mosquito bite.
   A linking
   B action

_____ 2. <u>Did</u> you <u>feel</u> that blast of cold air?
   A linking
   B action

_____ 3. Mr. Pacino <u>looks</u> much healthier now.
   A linking
   B action

_____ 4. Three people <u>were looking</u> for Kelly's contact lens.
   A linking
   B action

_____ 5. Inside the firehouse the alarm <u>sounded</u>.
   A linking
   B action

_____ 6. The sound system <u>sounded</u> a little better tonight.
   A linking
   B action

EXERCISEB Underline the verbs in the following sentences. Then label each one A for action or L for linking.

_____ 7. Must you turn the pages so quickly?

_____ 8. Suddenly three woodchucks appeared on the lawn.

_____ 9. Everyone at the party appears happy.

_____ 10. Did you smell those wild violets?

_____ 11. The grass smelled fresh after the rain.

_____ 12. Uncle Jarvis, the founder of a computer software company, had become a millionaire by his thirtieth birthday.

_____ 13. Irwin could have remained an engineer for the rest of his life.

CHAPTER 13 Distinguishing Between Linking Verbs and Action Verbs

EXERCISE Underline the verb in the following sentences. Write L in the blank if it is a linking verb or A if it is an action verb.

_____ 1. That must have been a very hungry mosquito.

_____ 2. That book about insects was Moira's.

_____ 3. We had not been close friends in Detroit.

_____ 4. The hikers climbed Pikes Peak in one day.

_____ 5. Annie will become a very competent engineer.

_____ 6. That unseeded watermelon smells very sweet.

_____ 7. The corn in the field grew quickly in the hot summer months.

_____ 8. The baby's hair remained blonde.

_____ 9. Mrs. Acheson's poodle dug up her prized tulips.

_____ 10. Broccoli with cheese or vinaigrette tastes very good.

_____ 11. I tasted Ms. Lin's egg drop soup.

_____ 12. The blue wig may look strange on you.

_____ 13. I quickly turned the page of the book.

_____ 14. The moon is full tonight.

_____ 15. Our next-door neighbor has been ill for a week.

_____ 16. Josh remained in the woods all night.

_____ 17. Owen has just become the club's president.

_____ 18. The comforter was hanging on the line.

_____ 19. The Minakos will be our new neighbors.

_____ 20. Alex handed his paper to the person behind him.

CHAPTER 13 Verbs Review

EXERCISEIdentify each underlined verb or verb phrase in the paragraph below.

Belinda **(1)** stomped into the living room and **(2)** put her hands on her hips. "This **(3)** is awful! Where are my keys?" she shouted. She **(4)** had searched her room top to bottom but **(5)** could not **(6)** find them anywhere. Just then she **(7)** heard a jingling sound and the front door **(8)** opened. Belinda's sister, Claire, **(9)** seemed amused as she walked in. She **(10)** pointed to the keys—Belinda's keys—hanging from the doorknob.

_____ 1. **A** helping verb
    B linking verb
    C transitive verb
    D intransitive verb

_____ 2. **A** helping verb
    B linking verb
    C transitive verb
    D intransitive verb

_____ 3. **A** helping verb
    B linking verb
    C transitive verb
    D intransitive verb

_____ 4. **A** helping verb
    B linking verb
    C transitive verb
    D intransitive verb

_____ 5. **A** helping verb
    B linking verb
    C transitive verb
    D intransitive verb

_____ 6. **A** helping verb
    B linking verb
    C transitive verb
    D intransitive verb

_____ 7. **A** helping verb
    B linking verb
    C transitive verb
    D intransitive verb

_____ 8. **A** helping verb
    B linking verb
    C transitive verb
    D intransitive verb

_____ 9. **A** helping verb
    B linking verb
    C transitive verb
    D intransitive verb

_____ 10. **A** helping verb
    B linking verb
    C transitive verb
    D intransitive verb

CHAPTER 14 Adjectives

[14A] An **adjective** is a word that modifies a noun or a pronoun.

EXERCISE A Identify the adjective from the choices following each sentence.

_____ 1. Do animals have natural enemies?
    A animals
    B have
    C natural
    D enemies

_____ 2. Strange friendships have occurred in the past.
    A Strange
    B friendships
    C occurred
    D past

_____ 3. A female cat adopted a tiny rat one day.
    A female
    B cat
    C rat
    D day

_____ 4. She treated it like a young kitten.
    A She
    B treated
    C like
    D young

_____ 5. Here we have another unusual combination.
    A Here
    B have
    C unusual
    D combination

EXERCISE B Underline the adjective or adjectives in each sentence.

6. There was a real rabbit at home.

7. The two animals became close friends.

8. A different dog befriended a skunk.

9. The timid koala lives in the outback of Australia.

10. The gentle koala is a very unsociable animal.

11. The koala can spend an entire lifetime in a secure treetop.

12. A wallaby is a sort of miniature kangaroo.

13. It is quite a shy animal also.

CHAPTER 14   Adjectives

EXERCISE Underline each adjective in the following sentences.

1. This restaurant is the best one in town.

2. Fifty soldiers stood in perfectly straight rows.

3. One koala saw a young wallaby.

4. It was a lonely baby by all accounts.

5. Tell me a scary story about ghosts and goblins!

6. I sank my teeth into the sweet cookie.

7. Wow! Taylor hit four home runs!

8. Rickie worked most weekends in June.

9. She earned high marks for her impressive performance.

10. These toys should be put in the big bin by the closet.

11. Someone finally turned off the loud alarm.

12. Janine, may I borrow your yellow highlighter?

13. The movie received many good reviews.

14. Michelle wore a red hat over her curly hair.

15. Few friends know my personal secrets.

16. We need fans in these empty bleachers!

17. Three kittens slept in a fuzzy pile.

18. Chad, please take more bread to the first table.

CHAPTER 14 Using Vivid Adjectives

EXERCISE Write a vivid adjective in the blank to complete each sentence.

1. The _____ building will be torn down soon.

2. I saw a _____ bird in that tree yesterday.

3. Do you want a _____ sweater for your birthday?

4. I enjoyed eating the _____ casserole.

5. _____ time was given for the assembly.

6. There was a(n) _____ crowd outside city hall.

7. Ellen's choice for a vacation was a _____ cross-country train trip.

8. She could easily be seen in her _____ coat.

9. Kent chose a(n) _____ book.

10. The _____ flowers decorated the table.

11. This is _____ work.

12. I was relieved to get the _____ beverage.

13. The children exhibited _____ behavior.

14. The room has a(n) _____ view.

15. The cook fed the group of _____ teenagers.

CHAPTER 14 Distinguishing Among Adjectives, Nouns, and Pronouns

---

EXERCISE A   Identify the underlined word in each sentence as an adjective, noun, or pronoun.

_____ 1. <u>That</u> was a delicious Sunday dinner.
   A adjective
   B noun
   C pronoun

_____ 2. That was a <u>delicious</u> Sunday dinner.
   A adjective
   B noun
   C pronoun

_____ 3. That restaurant has an unusual <u>dinner</u> menu.
   A adjective
   B noun
   C pronoun

_____ 4. <u>That</u> restaurant has an unusual dinner menu.
   A adjective
   B noun
   C pronoun

_____ 5. Those peculiar night sounds continue for <u>hours</u>.
   A adjective
   B noun
   C pronoun

_____ 6. <u>These</u> are the perfect curtains for my room.
   A adjective
   B noun
   C pronoun

EXERCISE B   Write whether the underlined word in each sentence is an adjective (A), noun (N), or pronoun (P).

_____ 7. All of the New York skyline disappeared in that <u>dense</u> fog.

_____ 8. All of the New York <u>skyline</u> disappeared in that dense fog.

_____ 9. Neither architect will visit any of the <u>building</u> sites until next week.

_____ 10. Neither <u>architect</u> will visit any of the building sites until next week.

_____ 11. <u>Some</u> of the older buildings had some noteworthy decorative features.

_____ 12. Some of the older <u>buildings</u> had some noteworthy decorative features.

_____ 13. Which steel beams are <u>those</u>?

_____ 14. Which <u>steel</u> beams are those?

CHAPTER 14 Identifying Adverbs

[14B] An **adverb** is a word that modifies a verb, an adjective, or another adverb.

EXERCISEUnderline the adverb in each sentence. Then choose the question that the adverb in the sentence answers.

_____ 1. Mitchell kicked the football hard.

    A Where?
    B When?
    C How?
    D To what extent?

_____ 2. Mitchell kicked the football yesterday.

    A Where?
    B When?
    C How?
    D To what extent?

_____ 3. Mitchell kicked the football around.

    A Where?
    B When?
    C How?
    D To what extent?

_____ 4. Mitchell kicked the football everywhere.

    A Where?
    B When?
    C How?
    D To what extent?

_____ 5. Mr. Chvany swept the stairs here.

    A Where?
    B When?
    C How?
    D To what extent?

_____ 6. Mr. Chvany finally swept the stairs.

    A Where?
    B When?
    C How?
    D To what extent?

_____ 7. Mr. Chvany swept the stairs well.

    A Where?
    B When?
    C How?
    D To what extent?

_____ 8. Mr. Chvany swept the very dirty stairs.

    A Where?
    B When?
    C How?
    D To what extent?

_____ 9. Mitchell kicked the football feebly.

    A Where?
    B When?
    C How?
    D To what extent?

_____ 10. Mitchell kicked the football outside.

    A Where?
    B When?
    C How?
    D To what extent?

_____ 11. Mitchell kicked the football earlier.

    A Where?
    B When?
    C How?
    D To what extent?

_____ 12. Mitchell kicked the football downstairs.

    A Where?
    B When?
    C How?
    D To what extent?

_____ 13. Mr. Chvany swept the stairs carefully.

    A Where?
    B When?
    C How?
    D To what extent?

_____ 14. Mr. Chvany swept the stairs today.

    A Where?
    B When?
    C How?
    D To what extent?

CHAPTER 14 Identifying Adverbs

EXERCISE Underline the adverb in each sentence.

1. The old train chugged forward.

2. The huge watchdog growled fiercely at the stranger.

3. I haven't seen that movie.

4. He often makes difficult decisions.

5. Julio will soon call his relatives in Mexico.

6. Our new cat seldom scratches people.

7. The small white plane landed safely.

8. Old houses are rapidly being remodeled.

9. We have hung festive decorations everywhere.

10. Was the full moon shining then?

11. Help me take these chairs inside, Phoebe.

12. The impatient man frequently checked his watch for the time.

13. Phina, Terry, and Lisa entered the speech contest yesterday.

14. I closed my eyes tightly against the bright sunlight.

15. Dad casually mentioned a birthday gift he had for me.

16. The doctor rarely took the subway to the hospital.

CHAPTER 14 Adverbs That Modify Verbs

EXERCISE A Select the adverb that modifies the underlined verb in each sentence.

_____ 1. Everyone <u>searched</u> carefully for the child.
   A Everyone
   B carefully
   C for
   D child

_____ 2. Maggie's watch <u>worked</u> perfectly this time.
   A Maggie's
   B watch
   C perfectly
   D this

_____ 3. Mr. Moon frequently <u>travels</u> to South Korea.
   A Mr. Moon
   B frequently
   C to
   D South Korea

_____ 4. Koala bears seldom <u>leave</u> their trees.
   A Koala
   B seldom
   C their
   D trees

_____ 5. The cloudy, dark sky <u>cleared</u> suddenly.
   A cloudy
   B dark
   C sky
   D suddenly

EXERCISE B Circle the adverb that modifies the underlined verb in each sentence.

6. A shooting star briefly <u>appeared</u> in the clear sky.

7. Soon the moon <u>disappeared</u> from everyone's view.

8. Sheila <u>moved</u> from Memphis to Chicago yesterday.

9. The audience <u>did</u> not <u>enjoy</u> the performance at the theater.

10. I <u>have</u> always <u>liked</u> country music and rockabilly.

11. Using long division Nate quickly <u>solved</u> the problem.

12. Danielle completely <u>forgot</u> about her biology test.

CHAPTER 14   Adverbs That Modify Verbs

EXERCISE A   Underline the adverb in each sentence. Then circle the verb it modifies.

1. Sarah actually enjoyed the difficult assignment.

2. The cat almost caught the young squirrel.

3. Bennie and I walked rapidly to the railway station from home.

4. Mrs. Dyer searched desperately for her briefcase.

5. Sometimes the telephone remains silent for hours.

6. The sturdy movers put the two tables there.

7. The raccoons were taken off the island immediately.

8. Carefully cut the bandage from the wound.

9. Kate answered each interview question knowledgeably.

EXERCISE B   Rewrite the following sentences, adding an adverb to modify the verb. Circle the adverb in the completed sentence.

10. My dog Abby jumps on people.

_____

11. She licks people's faces.

_____

12. Abby runs around the yard.

_____

13. She loves going for walks.

_____

14. She sleeps in my room.

_____

CHAPTER 14 Adverbs That Modify Verbs and Adjectives

EXERCISE A Choose the adverb or adverbs in each sentence.

_____ 1. Sometimes my little brother can be a big help.
  A little
  B big
  C little, big
  D Sometimes

_____ 2. We had one unusually cold day this June.
  A cold
  B this
  C unusually
  D unusually, this

_____ 3. Carlos is too fast for me.
  A for
  B fast
  C too, fast
  D too

_____ 4. That is a shockingly bright shade of purple.
  A shockingly
  B bright
  C purple
  D of, purple

_____ 5. Adam slept peacefully through the entire movie.
  A peacefully
  B through
  C entire
  D the, entire

EXERCISE B Underline the adverb or adverbs in each sentence.

6. She runs fast but can be quite clumsy with the ball.

7. Donna has just won the violin competition.

8. Complete eclipses occur rarely.

9. Her very thready pulse was beating rapidly.

10. The bull glared through the fence angrily.

11. Those are really beautiful flowers.

12. My brother and I never miss our favorite TV show.

13. Today we saw a truly great movie.

Name _____ Date _____

CHAPTER 14 **Adverbs That Modify Verbs, Adjectives, and Other Adverbs**

EXERCISE Decide whether the underlined adverb modifies a verb, an adjective, or an adverb.

_____ 1. The old bike works <u>surprisingly</u> well.
   A verb
   B adjective
   C adverb

_____ 2. The <u>extremely</u> nervous center fumbled the ball.
   A verb
   B adjective
   C adverb

_____ 3. That was a <u>rather</u> funny speech.
   A verb
   B adjective
   C adverb

_____ 4. The <u>exceptionally</u> long walk exhausted me.
   A verb
   B adjective
   C adverb

_____ 5. Read the directions <u>very</u> carefully.
   A verb
   B adjective
   C adverb

_____ 6. David arrived much <u>later</u> than Scott.
   A verb
   B adjective
   C adverb

_____ 7. The undertow was <u>alarmingly</u> strong.
   A verb
   B adjective
   C adverb

_____ 8. The job at the supermarket is <u>just</u> right for me.
   A verb
   B adjective
   C adverb

_____ 9. They were sitting <u>somewhat</u> close to the front.
   A verb
   B adjective
   C adverb

_____ 10. The river near our house seems <u>unusually</u> high.
   A verb
   B adjective
   C adverb

_____ 11. The temperature is falling <u>rather</u> quickly.
   A verb
   B adjective
   C adverb

_____ 12. My poison ivy is <u>extremely</u> itchy.
   A verb
   B adjective
   C adverb

_____ 13. Was the movie <u>very</u> funny?
   A verb
   B adjective
   C adverb

_____ 14. His predictions were <u>quite</u> accurate.
   A verb
   B adjective
   C adverb

Name _____ Date _____

CHAPTER 14 Adverbs That Modify Verbs, Adjectives, and Other Adverbs

EXERCISE Circle the word or words modified by the underlined adverb in each sentence.

1. Raccoons can <u>usually</u> thrive in suburban and urban settings.

2. Large numbers of them <u>often</u> gather for nightly feedings at garbage cans.

3. They may seem like <u>perfectly</u> adorable pets.

4. Sometimes young raccoons behave in a <u>quite</u> friendly manner, but they will always remain wild animals.

5. <u>Now</u> raccoons are presenting a serious new threat.

6. They are <u>partially</u> responsible for an alarming rise in the incidence of rabies.

7. An epidemic is highly unlikely, but some danger <u>certainly</u> exists.

8. Rabies is <u>nearly</u> always fatal and cannot be treated in animals.

9. It can be almost <u>totally</u> prevented by immunization.

10. Raccoon rabies spreads <u>fairly</u> easily to dogs and cats.

11. Many health officials <u>now</u> require the vaccination of dogs and cats.

12. They are also asking that people report all <u>seemingly</u> ill animals and all bites.

Name _____   Date _____

CHAPTER 14 — Adjectives and Adverbs Review

EXERCISE Identify each underlined word in the paragraph below.

Have you **(1)** <u>ever</u> wondered about the **(2)** <u>first</u> words spoken on the moon? **(3)** <u>Almost</u> everyone knows that astronaut Neil Armstrong said, "That's one **(4)** <u>small</u> step for man, one giant leap for mankind." **(5)** <u>This</u> means that Armstrong's step from **(6)** <u>the</u> lunar lander to the lunar surface represents a supreme achievement for the **(7)** <u>human</u> species. What is a less **(8)** <u>well-known</u> fact, however, is that Armstrong misspoke when he said those first words on the moon. Knowing he would go down in **(9)** <u>American</u> history must have made Armstrong nervous. He **(10)** <u>actually</u> meant to say, "That's one small step for **(11)** <u>a</u> man."

_____ 1. **A** proper adjective
B compound adjective
C article
D adverb

_____ 2. **A** compound adjective
B adverb
C adjective
D proper adjective

_____ 3. **A** pronoun
B adjective
C adverb
D article

_____ 4. **A** adverb
B compound adjective
C adjective
D noun

_____ 5. **A** proper adjective
B pronoun
C adjective
D adverb

_____ 6. **A** article
B proper adjective
C compound adjective
D adverb

_____ 7. **A** adjective
B noun
C adverb
D article

_____ 8. **A** adverb
B compound adjective
C proper adjective
D article

_____ 9. **A** proper adjective
B noun
C article
D adverb

_____ 10. **A** proper adjective
B adjective
C article
D adverb

_____ 11. **A** pronoun
B compound adjective
C adverb
D article

CHAPTER 15 Prepositions

[15A] A **preposition** is a word that shows the relationship between a noun or a pronoun and another word in the sentence.

EXERCISE Underline the preposition or prepositions in each sentence.

1. Most eagles fly with their wings.

2. These newborn eaglets flew by plane.

3. People gathered excitedly at the airport.

4. They cheered the arrival of the baby birds.

5. The birds were transported from Canada.

6. They were a gift to Massachusetts.

7. The bald eagle is a symbol of the United States.

8. Many eagles live in remote areas.

9. These eaglets will be raised on Massachusetts land.

10. Thirty feet above the ground, a nest was built.

11. Guards will stay posted near the nest.

12. Until July the birds will be fed by hand.

13. Then they will soar high into the air.

14. They will fly far beyond the nest.

15. After four years they may return and raise their own eaglets.

CHAPTER 15 Prelpositions

CHAPTER 15 Prepositions

EXERCISE A Select the preposition that fills in the blank of each sentence.

_____ 1. The bushes _____ the house need trimming.
   A on
   B throughout
   C growing
   D beside

_____ 2. Frank should go _____ the store.
   A running
   B to
   C till
   D aside from

_____ 3. The package _____ the chair is mine.
   A during
   B by means of
   C sitting
   D on

_____ 4. We should not go _____ the storm.
   A into
   B like
   C in place of
   D driving

_____ 5. Ken hid _____ the boat.
   A instead of
   B of
   C inside
   D rowing

EXERCISE B Fill in the blank with an appropriate preposition. There may be more than one answer that makes sense.

6. Gloria will attend the meeting _____ Howard.

7. The ball rolled _____ the street.

8. Janet walked _____ the water.

9. Carl sat _____ Marcy at the game.

10. The plane flew _____ the storm clouds.

11. Place these books _____ the bookends.

12. A little squirrel scampered _____ the large oak tree.

13. I have been tired _____ lunchtime.

Name _____   Date _____

CHAPTER 15 Prepositional Phrases

[15A.2] A prepositional **phrase** begins with a preposition and ends with a noun or a pronoun.

EXERCISE A Choose the prepositional phrase in each sentence.

_____ 1. Rishu planned a cookout with her family.
   A planned a cookout
   B cookout with her
   C with her family
   D Rishu planned

_____ 2. They set the barbecue grill in their backyard.
   A their backyard
   B in their backyard
   C set the barbecue grill
   D in their back

_____ 3. Rishu's mom placed meat inside a covered dish.
   A inside a covered dish
   B meat inside
   C placed meat
   D a covered dish

_____ 4. Rishu put the covered dish next to the grill.
   A dish next to
   B put the covered dish
   C to the grill
   D next to the grill

_____ 5. Rishu's dad flavored the meat according to his secret recipe.
   A according to his secret recipe
   B to his secret
   C flavored the meat
   D his secret recipe

EXERCISE B Underline the prepositional phrase in each sentence.

6. In addition to the meat, Rishu's family would cook potatoes.

7. Rishu wrapped clean potatoes inside aluminum foil.

8. The potatoes would be cooked by means of hot coals.

9. Rishu's dad put the potatoes underneath hot coals.

10. The potatoes would bake because of the heat.

11. Rishu looked inside the refrigerator.

12. She found the ketchup and mustard behind the pickles.

CHAPTER 15 Prepositional Phrases

EXERCISE On the lines below, write the prepositional phrase or phrases from each sentence of the paragraph.

(1) Here is a recipe for spicy scrambled eggs. (2) You will need six eggs, a small onion, a tomato, a garlic clove, a pinch of red pepper flakes, and a tablespoon of oil. (3) Break each of the eggs into a bowl. (4) Beat the eggs with a fork or with a whisk. (5) On a cutting board, chop the onion and garlic into small pieces. (6) Boil some water in a pot on the stove. (7) Drop the tomato into the boiling water. (8) Count to twelve. (9) Remove the tomato from the pot with a slotted spoon. (10) Pull the skin off the tomato. (11) Cut it into small pieces. (12) Heat the oil in a frying pan. (13) Add the onion, garlic, and red pepper flakes to the pan. (14) After five minutes, add the eggs and chopped tomato. (15) Cook for three to five minutes.

1. _____
2. _____
3. _____
4. _____
5. _____
6. _____
7. _____
8. _____
9. _____
10. _____
11. _____
12. _____
13. _____
14. _____
15. _____

CHAPTER 15 Prepositions and Adverbs

ExerciseA   Write P if the underlined word is a preposition or A if it is an adverb.

_____ 1. <u>After</u> dinner Jake put his costume away.

_____ 2. The sun came up <u>at</u> five.

_____ 3. A caterpillar crawled <u>down</u> my leg.

_____ 4. <u>Along</u> the bank grew masses of cattails.

_____ 5. We rested <u>under</u> a large oak tree.

_____ 6. "Please move <u>along</u>," requested the police officer.

_____ 7. They went <u>in</u> and bought tickets.

_____ 8. They looked <u>in</u> the box but found nothing.

_____ 9. Hannah waited <u>inside</u> because of the rain.

_____ 10. <u>On</u> his head the ram had two curved horns.

EXERCISEB   Underline each preposition, and circle each adverb in the sentences below.

11. Walk the pony around the rink.

12. "Be careful that you don't fall off," he shouted.

13. Everyone sang as the flag went up.

14. George did his exercises before breakfast.

15. If you go outside, take your key.

16. Up the hill raced the boys on their bikes.

17. All the marbles rolled off the table.

18. We looked around but couldn't find them.

19. Haven't I met you before?

20. The suitcases can be stored underneath the seats.

CHAPTER 15   Finding Conjunctions

[15B] A **conjunction** connects words or groups of words.

EXERCISE A   Select the conjunction or conjunctions in each sentence.

_____ 1. Clocks and watches are sold in that store.
    A and
    B are
    C in
    D that

_____ 2. Neither Elena nor her sister was at school today.
    A Neither / nor
    B nor
    C was
    D today

_____ 3. The needle jumped and skipped on the old record.
    A needle
    B jumped
    C and
    D on

_____ 4. Both the washing machine and the dryer are in use now.
    A Both
    B Both / and
    C are
    D now

_____ 5. Does anyone have a needle or a safety pin?
    A anyone
    B a
    C or
    D pin

_____ 6. Wild blueberries are small but delicious.
    A Wild
    B are
    C small
    D but

EXERCISE B   Write the conjunction or conjunctions in each sentence.

_____ 7. The wind and rain continued all night.

_____ 8. Two cars did skid but didn't crash.

_____ 9. The new student's name is either Leroy or Larry.

_____ 10. The shoes are on sale not only today but also tomorrow.

_____ 11. We looked for her keys in the house and on the lawn.

_____ 12. The alarm didn't go off, so I was late for school.

_____ 13. I will go with either Nancy or her sister.

CHAPTER 15   Conjunctions and the Words They Connect

EXERCISE Circle the conjunctions in the following sentences, and underline the words each conjunction connects.

1. Hillary and Dora drew the art show posters.

2. The judge pronounced a severe but fair sentence.

3. Slowly but steadily the lion stalked the deer.

4. Either they or we will carry the banner in the parade.

5. Four of the guests arrived early and left late.

6. The spaghetti slid out of the bowl and onto the floor.

7. Franklin School won not only the game but also the championship.

8. Our team was ahead, but our lead was a narrow one.

9. We searched for the missing earring both at school and at home.

10. Detective Brien had interviewed everyone, yet she was still puzzled.

CHAPTER 15 Determining Parts of Speech

EXERCISE A Select the correct part of speech of the underlined word in each sentence.

_____ 1. The <u>windows</u> gleamed in the sun.
  A noun
  B verb

_____ 2. The door is <u>open</u>.
  A noun
  B adjective

_____ 3. Carry the dish <u>carefully</u>.
  A adjective
  B adverb

_____ 4. Is <u>he</u> going to India?
  A pronoun
  B preposition

_____ 5. <u>Somebody</u> turned off the light.
  A pronoun
  B noun

_____ 6. Mr. Sharp <u>fed</u> the pigeons daily.
  A adverb
  B verb

_____ 7. Are Kelly's eyes green <u>or</u> blue?
  A conjunction
  B adjective

_____ 8. <u>Good</u>! You sewed on the button.
  A noun
  B interjection

EXERCISE B Write the part of speech of the underlined word in each sentence.

_____ 9. The dog barked <u>at</u> the noisy truck.

_____ 10. People entered and looked <u>around</u>.

_____ 11. <u>She</u> took the bus to Columbus Avenue.

_____ 12. David <u>invited</u> twelve people to the party.

_____ 13. <u>Careful</u>! The traffic light hasn't changed yet.

_____ 14. The tiny dog made a <u>huge</u> racket.

_____ 15. <u>That</u> is Sally's record.

_____ 16. The damaged plane landed <u>in</u> a field.

CHAPTER 15 Finding Parts of Speech

> **EXERCISE** Choose the answer that fi ts the part of speech given in parentheses for each sentence.

_____ 1. (adverb) The man on the movie screen screamed horribly.

    A man
    B movie
    C screamed
    D horribly

_____ 2. (verb) The ninth grade eats lunch at 12:30 every day.

    A eats
    B lunch
    C 12:30
    D day

_____ 3. (adjective) The sky had a rosy glow in the evening.

    A sky
    B rosy
    C glow
    D evening

_____ 4. (noun) This is my favorite holiday.

    A This
    B my
    C favorite
    D holiday

_____ 5. (interjection) Ugh! That pear was too mushy.

    A Ugh!
    B That
    C too
    D mushy

_____ 6. (pronoun) Did she buy the yellow sweater?

    A Did
    B she
    C yellow
    D sweater

_____ 7. (preposition) That book is by Herman Melville.

    A That
    B book
    C by
    D Melville

_____ 8. (conjunction) The sky looked dark and stormy all afternoon.

    A sky
    B looked
    C and
    D all

_____ 9. (pronoun) Nobody needed a hammer or nails.

    A Nobody
    B needed
    C hammer
    D or

_____ 10. (adverb) I have definitely made my decision.

    A I
    B definitely
    C my
    D decision

_____ 11. (adverb) I do not approve of the new school policy.

    A do
    B not
    C new
    D school

_____ 12. (noun) She asked him for a specific answer to a difficult question.

    A asked
    B specific
    C answer
    D difficult

CHAPTER 15 Finding Parts of Speech

> **EXERCISE** Underline the word or words that fi t the part of speech given in parentheses for each sentence.

1. (pronoun) Those were the best soccer games I had ever played.

2. (verb) We carefully backed into the garage filled with bicycles and sports equipment.

3. (adjective) Jamie carved a hiking stick from the oak branch.

4. (conjunction) I thought we were finished, but we had plenty of work ahead of us.

5. (preposition) Prior to the big event, we were very excited.

6. (noun) Before my grandparents arrived, I vacuumed the living room.

7. (pronoun) That is the reason we studied so hard.

8. (verb) I thought that my thoughts on the subject were valid.

9. (adjective) My mother told me to sweep the back stairwell.

10. (adverb) Lately I have been collecting stamps and coins.

11. (conjunction) Not only am I tired, but also I am hungry.

12. (preposition) Raghu flew the remote control plane around the elm tree.

CHAPTER 15   Other Parts of Speech Review

EXERCISE Identify each underlined word or phrase in the paragraph below.

Tia **(1)** and her dad took a football **(2)** to the park to throw around. It was a crisp fall morning **(3)** with crunchy leaves on the ground. The sun came **(4)** out of the clouds by midday, warming the air. **(5)** Both Tia and her dad were getting hungry, **(6)** so they walked over to a food cart. **(7)** According to the sign, they could get two hot dogs **(8)** for three dollars. "**(9)** Yum!" Tia said after taking a bite **(10)** of her hot dog.

_____ 1. **A** interjection
   B preposition
   C correlative conjunction
   D conjunction

_____ 2. **A** prepositional phrase
   B compound preposition
   C correlative conjunction
   D preposition

_____ 3. **A** interjection
   B compound preposition
   C conjunction
   D preposition

_____ 4. **A** prepositional phrase
   B compound preposition
   C correlative conjunction
   D conjunction

_____ 5. **A** prepositional phrase
   B compound preposition
   C correlative conjunction
   D conjunction

_____ 6. **A** conjunction
   B preposition
   C correlative conjunction
   D interjection

_____ 7. **A** prepositional phrase
   B compound preposition
   C correlative conjunction
   D interjection

_____ 8. **A** prepositional phrase
   B compound preposition
   C correlative conjunction
   D preposition

_____ 9. **A** conjunction
   B compound preposition
   C interjection
   D preposition

_____ 10. **A** correlative conjunction
   B preposition
   C interjection
   D conjunction

CHAPTER 16 Recognizing Sentences and Fragments

[16A] A **sentence** is a group of words that expresses a complete thought.

[16A.1] A group of words that expresses an incomplete thought is a **sentencefragment** .

EXERCISE Write S if the word group is a sentence or F if it is a sentence fragment.

_____ 1. Sent the package to her yesterday.

_____ 2. A history teacher at the middle school.

_____ 3. Roberto works on Saturday afternoons.

_____ 4. Skied down a mountain for the first time.

_____ 5. Since are going out for dinner.

_____ 6. George does twenty push-ups each morning.

_____ 7. Laughed at Antonia's jokes.

_____ 8. The corn is planted in the far field.

_____ 9. Feeds the ducks while her mother watches.

_____ 10. Luis bought a 3-D puzzle of a castle.

_____ 11. On Saturday afternoons Shaniqua practices the flute.

_____ 12. Walks toward the stables in the rain.

_____ 13. I saw you for the first time in seventh grade.

_____ 14. Phil gave Tariq some tips on making a Web site.

_____ 15. Sharpened pencils for the geometry test.

CHAPTER 16 Recognizing Sentences and Fragments

EXERCISE Rewrite each sentence fragment it to make it a complete sentence.

1. Because shouldn't look directly at an eclipse of the sun.

   _____

2. Solved the crime last month.

   _____

3. The cute dog that lives next door.

   _____

4. Lifted weights at the gym.

   _____

5. Two possible answers to the question.

   _____

6. Buys a new CD on the Internet.

   _____

7. Scored a basket in the last two seconds of the game.

   _____

8. Before anyone else in the house.

   _____

9. A skilled heart surgeon named Dr. Sanchez.

   _____

CHAPTER 16   Simple Subjects

[16B] The **subject** names the person, place, thing, or idea that the sentence is about.
[16B.2] A **simplesubject** is the main word in the complete subject.

EXERCISE Write the simple subject in each sentence.

_____   1. The bus was late again.

_____   2. My uncle arrived yesterday.

_____   3. Her dress was pink and purple.

_____   4. Victor caught two small fish.

_____   5. Elvis Presley lived in Memphis, Tennessee.

_____   6. You cannot use that entrance.

_____   7. The playful kitten chased the string.

_____   8. The gray kitten seems lost.

_____   9. The striped snake lay hidden.

_____   10. His new shoe hurt his big toe.

_____   11. Two socks were left in the gym.

_____   12. Two red socks lay under the bed.

_____   13. The bridge was damaged by the storm.

_____   14. A house on Arch Road was flooded.

_____   15. The bumps in the road can damage the car.

_____   16. The girl with long, red hair is my cousin.

_____   17. The young boy with black hair is Sam Tiner.

_____   18. Your books are on the table.

_____   19. His pictures of Rosa are too dark.

_____   20. Lisa's pictures are too light.

CHAPTER 16 **Complete Subjects**

[16B.1] A **completesubject** includes all the words used to identify the person, place, thing, or idea that the sentence is about.

EXERCISEUnderline the complete subject in each sentence.

---

1. The bus was late again.

2. My uncle arrived yesterday.

3. Her dress was pink and purple.

4. Victor caught two small fish.

5. Elvis Presley lived in Memphis, Tennessee.

6. You cannot use that entrance.

7. The kitten chased the string.

8. The gray kitten seems lost.

9. The striped snake lay hidden.

10. His new shoe hurt his big toe.

11. Two socks were left in the gym.

12. Two red socks lay under the bed.

13. The bridge was damaged by the storm.

14. A house on Arch Road was flooded.

15. The bumps in the road can damage the car.

16. The boy with red hair is my cousin.

17. The young boy with red hair is Sam.

18. Your pictures are on the table.

19. Your pictures of Rosa are too dark.

20. Lisa's pictures are too light.

CHAPTER 16 Complete Subjects

EXERCISE On the lines below, write the complete subject for each sentence of the paragraph.

(1) Christopher Columbus made his famous voyage to the New World in 1492. (2) His goal was actually to find a short route to the West Indies. (3) He had a daring and expensive plan. (4) The result of his voyage is well known.

(5) Columbus made a triumphant return from the New World to Spain in 1493. (6) A second voyage was organized immediately. (7) The first colony in America was founded on that trip. (8) Many of the colonists complained about the settlement and Columbus. (9) The early settlers had expected easy conditions and immediate wealth.

(10) The great Italian explorer died in 1506 after four difficult voyages to the New World.

1. _____

2. _____

3. _____

4. _____

5. _____

6. _____

7. _____

8. _____

9. _____

10. _____

CHAPTER 16   Simple Predicates

[16B] The **predicate** tells something about the subject.

[16B.4] A **simplepredicate** , or **verb**, is the main word or phrase in the complete predicate.

EXERCISEUnderline the simple predicate in each sentence.

---

1. My aunt travels often.

2. She designs luggage.

3. Her job takes her everywhere.

4. People in Asia use her suitcases.

5. Travelers in Europe carry them.

6. The suitcases are strong.

7. They are very light as well.

8. Such qualities make them popular.

9. Aunt Alice is in Egypt now.

10. That nation lies mainly in Africa.

11. A small part extends into Asia.

12. Egypt receives very little rain.

13. Deserts cover most of the land.

14. The deserts form part of the Sahara.

15. Egypt has had a long history.

16. The dry air has preserved many of the ancient monuments.

17. Many ancient treasures have been found there.

18. My aunt will visit the pyramids.

19. She is returning next week.

20. She must travel to China next.

CHAPTER 16 Complete Predicates

[16B.3] A **completepredicate** includes all the words that tell what the subject is doing or that tell something about the subject.

EXERCISEA Choose the complete predicate in each sentence.

_____ 1. Stickball games could be found in almost every neighborhood in New York fifty years ago.
    A could be found in almost every neighborhood in New York fifty years ago
    B could be found in almost every neighborhood

_____ 2. The city streets echoed with the sounds of the game.
    A echoed with the sounds
    B echoed with the sounds of the game

_____ 3. The game is an old one.
    A is
    B is an old one

_____ 4. It is similar to softball.
    A is similar to softball
    B is similar

_____ 5. Now the game has almost disappeared from the streets.
    A has almost disappeared from the streets
    B has almost disappeared

EXERCISEB Underline the complete predicate in each sentence.

6. A few players do sometimes relive the good old days.

7. A gray-haired man slammed the ball with a broomstick.

8. He slid swiftly onto a mark near the curb.

9. He and his friends had last played stickball forty years ago.

10. They and the city looked different then.

11. Jimmy Dale Gilmore and the Flatlanders came to play at our high school.

12. Yesterday I jogged and studied for my algebra exam before breakfast.

13. Johnny and my sister Veda organized this year's first poetry and fiction reading.

14. I have not heard anything about the parade.

CHAPTER 16 Verb Phrases

[16B.5] A **verbphrase** includes the main verb plus any helping, or auxiliary, verbs.

EXERCISEA Select the verb phrase for each sentence.

_____ 1. The first photograph was taken in 1826.
  A was
  B taken in 1826
  C photograph
  D was taken

_____ 2. The freshman class election results will be announced on Monday.
  A election results
  B will be announced
  C will be
  D announced

_____ 3. Dandelion leaves can be eaten raw like lettuce.
  A like lettuce
  B can be
  C can be eaten
  D eaten raw

_____ 4. Their sneakers are drying in the sun.
  A are drying
  B drying in the sun
  C are
  D Their sneakers

_____ 5. The invitation must have given the time.
  A must have
  B given the time
  C must have given
  D have given

_____ 6. You should have spoken to me first.
  A should have
  B to me first
  C spoken
  D should have spoken

EXERCISEB Write the verb phrase in each sentence.

_____ 7. The Girl Scouts was founded on March 12, 1912.

_____ 8. American Indians could make beads from shells.

_____ 9. The award should have gone to her.

_____ 10. With help babies can swim at an early age.

_____ 11. I must have lost the keys to the house.

_____ 12. Some parts of Brazil have never been explored.

CHAPTER 16 Compound Subjects

[16B.6] A **compoundsubject** is two or more subjects in one sentence that have the same verb and are joined by a conjunction.

EXERCISE Underline the compound subject in each sentence.

1. Spices and herbs improve the taste of food.

2. Many CDs and DVDs will be on sale at Diskette's next week.

3. Blizzards, hurricanes, and floods hit New England this year.

4. The captain and his crew stayed with the damaged vessel.

5. My older sister and my brother play the electric guitar.

6. Carla, Joyce, and Juan were elected the new class officers.

7. Both Kim and Lila tried out for lead roles in the play.

8. Either a turkey or a goose will be part of our Thanksgiving meal.

9. Grandparents, parents, and children gathered for the reunion.

10. Neither snow nor sleet stops our mail carrier.

11. Hikers and cyclists often camp by the brook.

12. Neither Gladys nor Rosalie can babysit for us.

13. The best baseballs and footballs are made of leather.

14. Shells, starfish, and driftwood are among her souvenirs.

15. Insects and disease are the major enemies of trees.

16. My family and I will fly to Arizona next week.

17. *Jane, Jean,* and *Joan* are forms of the same ancient name.

18. Both basketball and volleyball were first played in the state of Massachusetts.

19. Carnations and zinnias last a long time.

20. Breakfast, lunch, and dinner were included in the price.

CHAPTER 16   Compound Verbs

[16B.7] A **compoundverb** is formed when two or more verbs in one sentence have the same subject and are joined by a conjunction.

EXERCISE Select the compound verb for each sentence.

_____ 1. My cousin Ida dived into the pool and injured her arm.
  A dived
  B dived, injured
  C pool
  D dived, pool, injured

_____ 2. I slipped and tumbled down the stairs.
  A tumbled
  B slipped, down
  C slipped, tumbled
  D slipped, tumbled, stairs

_____ 3. The nurse arrived and noticed the improvement.
  A nurse, arrived, noticed
  B arrived, noticed
  C noticed
  D noticed, improvement

_____ 4. Bradley told jokes and entertained everyone.
  A told, entertained
  B told, jokes
  C jokes, entertained
  D told, jokes, entertained

_____ 5. The tired dancer lay on the mat and exhaled slowly.
  A tired, dancer, lay
  B lay, mat, exhaled
  C dancer, lay, exhaled
  D lay, exhaled

_____ 6. She caught the bus or took a taxi.
  A caught, took
  B bus, took
  C bus, taxi
  D caught, bus, taxi

_____ 7. Mr. Lee ran to the phone, inserted a coin, and called the police.
  A ran, inserted
  B ran, phone, inserted
  C ran, phone, inserted, coin
  D ran, inserted, called

_____ 8. Kathleen views the calm blue sea and is content.
  A views, sea
  B views, is
  C calm, sea
  D views, content

_____ 9. The detective suspected the secretary but interviewed everyone.
  A suspected, interviewed
  B suspected, everyone
  C detective, interviewed
  D interviewed

_____ 10. My doctor opened an office but needs more space.
  A opened
  B opened, needs
  C opened, space
  D office, needs

CHAPTER 16 Compound Verbs

EXERCISE Write *YES* if the sentence has a compound verb. Write *NO* if the sentence does not have a compound verb.

_____ 1. This year's winter winds were swift and cold.

_____ 2. The horse leapt the fence and raced across the open field.

_____ 3. Lorenzo runs the cash register, wipes the counters, and stocks supplies.

_____ 4. By the end of the game, the players were tired but proud.

_____ 5. I bought the hiking boots but returned the compass to the shelf.

_____ 6. Tamara and Emily went to Mindy's house for the afternoon.

_____ 7. Nick called Dakota on the telephone but wrote Kyle an email.

_____ 8. Play fairly or leave the game.

_____ 9. The roller coaster crested the top of the hill.

_____ 10. After school that day, Lidon cycled up the steep hill and coasted down the other side.

_____ 11. Note cards or some other form of documentation is necessary.

_____ 12. The happy puppy rolled and kicked his legs in the air.

_____ 13. Ms. Nguyen raised her hands, quieted the class, and began her lesson.

_____ 14. Bees and butterflies floated and fluttered in the summer breeze.

_____ 15. Marie opened a Web page and viewed the contents.

CHAPTER 16   Compound Verbs

EXERCISE Underline the compound verb in each sentence.

1. We painted the vase and then fired it in the kiln.

2. My math book fell off my desk and thudded on the floor.

3. Jesse's remote control car raced down the street and jumped the ramp.

4. Kerri used a charcoal pencil and then chose several colored pencils.

5. Mr. Sizemore, the chef, grilled meat and steamed vegetables.

6. The planetarium opens early but closes early as well.

7. Our veterinarian has lots of experience and is gentle with animals.

8. Either buy the magazine or put it back on the shelf.

9. We attended Zeke's Bar Mitzvah and enjoyed ourselves.

10. Charles first chose woodworking class but later transferred to shop.

11. Joanna swims and dives every day.

12. The singer practiced her solo and waited for her stage call.

CHAPTER 16 · Compound Subjects and Compound Verbs

EXERCISE Write CS if the sentence has a compound subject, CV if it has a compound verb, or B if it has both a compound subject and a compound verb.

_____ 1. Neither the farmer nor his young helper could budge the bull.

_____ 2. Two woodchucks, four rabbits, and a raccoon waited outside the fence and stared at the gardeners.

_____ 3. A blue pair and a green pair of earmuffs were found on the beach.

_____ 4. My brothers and my younger sister accompanied me to the bookstore and to the computer shop and helped me with my selections.

_____ 5. The meeting of molecular biologists is usually held in Chicago but will be held in Houston this year.

_____ 6. Not only fleas but also ticks are attacking both the dog and the cat.

_____ 7. The tattered, tired traveler arrived home and ate supper.

_____ 8. An important set of keys and a box of confidential files had been missing but were finally discovered behind a file cabinet.

_____ 9. This person and that one must certainly be your relatives.

_____ 10. Neither the seal nor the walrus would obey the trainer, perform for the crowd, or even be bribed with pieces of raw fish.

_____ 11. A bat and a ball are used in the game of cricket.

_____ 12. Cricket is popular in England and is played in a few other countries.

_____ 13. Cricket and baseball are similar games.

_____ 14. One player pitches or bowls a ball.

_____ 15. A player on the opposite team hits the ball and scores runs.

_____ 16. Players in cricket do not have bases but use two wickets instead.

_____ 17. The batsman and the bowler stand at opposite wickets and face each other.

_____ 18. A match may continue for several days and involve hundreds of runs.

_____ 19. Cricket may have been played in the 1300s but did not become a major sport until the 1700s.

_____ 20. Both baseball and cricket have complicated rules but are enjoyed by many people.

Name _____ Date _____

CHAPTER 16 **Compound Subjects and Compound Verbs**

EXERCISEA Decide whether each sentence has a compound subject, compound verb, or both.

_____ 1. Card games and puzzles entertained the children during the long afternoon.
  A compound subject
  B compound verb
  C both

_____ 2. The fickle sun shone brightly and then hid behind clouds.
  A compound subject
  B compound verb
  C both

_____ 3. Either Paula or Ms. Rodniszky adopted the golden retriever.
  A compound subject
  B compound verb
  C both

_____ 4. Campers and hikers blazed the trail and kept it free of litter.
  A compound subject
  B compound verb
  C both

_____ 5. Neither pesticides nor chemicals are used on these organic vegetables.
  A compound subject
  B compound verb
  C both

_____ 6. Ants and flies found their way to our picnic and helped themselves to our food.
  A compound subject
  B compound verb
  C both

EXERCISEB Underline each compound subject and circle each compound verb in the following paragraph.

(1) Jim Lewis and Jim Springer are twins but were adopted by different parents. **(2)** They had neither met nor talked to each other for 30 years. **(3)** Some unusual facts were then discovered and explored.

(4) Lewis's wife and Springer's wife were both named Betty. **(5)** James Allen and James Alan were the names of their first sons. **(6)** Math and woodworking were hobbies of both brothers. **(7)** The twins drove the same make of car and had vacationed at the same beach in Florida. **(8)** These similarities may seem unreal and sound like coincidences. **(9)** However, some researchers and scientists don't think so.

(10) They have now found identical brainwave patterns in twins and discovered other similarities.

56 Grade 9 • Chapter 16: The Sentence Base   Copyright © Perfection Learning® All rights reserved.

CHAPTER 16 Natural and Inverted Order

[16B.8] When the subject in a sentence comes before the verb, the sentence is in **naturalorder** . When the verb or part of a verb phrase comes before the subject, the sentence is in **invertedorder** .

EXERCISE Write N if the sentence is in natural order or I if it is in inverted order.

_____ 1. Can you see her in the crowd?

_____ 2. There goes the last hamburger.

_____ 3. The registration booth is over here.

_____ 4. Here are the muffins and bagels.

_____ 5. Did your teacher give you a choice of subjects?

_____ 6. The treasure hunter did not find buried treasure on the island.

_____ 7. I did answer the question correctly.

_____ 8. There are four taste sensations: sweet, bitter, sour, and salty.

_____ 9. Over the waves roared the speedboat.

_____ 10. Philippa planted rosebushes along the garden wall.

_____ 11. High on the mountain stood the hikers.

_____ 12. The ground began to tremble beneath our feet.

_____ 13. Between Las Vegas and Barstow lies a great desert.

_____ 14. Where is the surprise?

_____ 15. Here is the book report for you to read.

Grade 9 • Chapter 16: The Sentence Base **57**

CHAPTER 16 Writing Sentences in Inverted Order

EXERCISE Rewrite each sentence in inverted order.

1. The rake lay under the pile of leaves.

   _____

2. Oscar's pet chameleon crawled out of the kitchen window.

   _____

3. That noisy, low-flying plane is coming again.

   _____

4. The programs for the play are there.

   _____

5. You are feeling how?

   _____

6. Grandma and Grandpa are coming when?

   _____

7. Too many desserts are there.

   _____

8. The experiment failed for what reason?

   _____

9. A beeping sound came from the computer.

   _____

10. A furry spider scurried under the table.

   _____

11. How beautiful you are!

   _____

Name _____ Date _____

Writing Sentences in Inverted Order

EXERCISE A Each sentence is written in inverted order. Choose the subject and verb of each sentence.

_____ 1. Why can't Clara bring the records?
- **A** Clara, can bring
- **B** records, bring
- **C** Why, can bring
- **D** Clara, records

_____ 2. Around the track raced the motorcycles.
- **A** track, raced
- **B** motorcycles, around
- **C** track, motorcycles
- **D** motorcycles, raced

_____ 3. When did Joshua arrive at the party?
- **A** When, did arrive
- **B** When, Joshua
- **C** Joshua, did arrive
- **D** arrive, party

_____ 4. In the clear blue sky appeared a single rain cloud.
- **A** single, appeared
- **B** cloud, appeared
- **C** sky, appeared
- **D** blue, appeared

_____ 5. Over the fence darted the stealthy cat.
- **A** fence, cat
- **B** cat, darted
- **C** Over, darted
- **D** stealthy, cat

_____ 6. There is a contest for short story writers.
- **A** contest, is
- **B** There, is
- **C** writers, is
- **D** story, is

EXERCISE B Each sentence is written in inverted order. Underline the subject and circle the verb in each sentence.

7. Why did the dog bark in the night?

8. When will the mariachi band arrive?

9. Inside the cover was the author's autograph.

10. Here is a beautiful yet affordable necklace.

11. Out of the sky fell golf-ball-sized hail.

12. How did you do on the test?

CHAPTER 16   Understood Subjects

[16B.9] When the subject of a sentence is not stated, the subject is an **understood** *you*.

> **EXERCISE**Write *YES* if the sentence has an understood subject. Write *NO* if the sentence does not have an understood subject.

_____ 1. Take the dog for a walk.

_____ 2. Lend me your notes from math class.

_____ 3. Michael, carry these packages for me.

_____ 4. Here comes dinner right now.

_____ 5. Get some milk at the store.

_____ 6. Leave the keys on the table.

_____ 7. Has Roger spoken to you about the meeting?

_____ 8. Carly, meet me at three o'clock.

_____ 9. Answer the questions very carefully.

_____ 10. Into the gym raced the eager players.

_____ 11. Look up the word in the dictionary, please.

_____ 12. Where are the magazines I bought?

_____ 13. Ms. Vega, please give me a hall pass.

_____ 14. At the end of class, return the paintbrushes to this cabinet.

_____ 15. Why is the sky blue?

_____ 16. Will you teach me karate?

_____ 17. Rachel, you are a fantastic friend!

_____ 18. First, pick up our mail at the post office.

_____ 19. Watch the baby for me this afternoon.

_____ 20. Back up each computer file frequently.

• • • CHAPTER 16   Direct Objects

[16C] A **complement** is a word or group of words that completes the meaning of subjects or verbs.

[16C.1] A **directobject** is a noun or pronoun that receives the action of the verb.

> **EXERCISE** Choose the direct object(s), if any, in each sentence.

_____ 1. Someone finally found Hank's book.
- **A** Hank's
- **B** Someone
- **C** book
- **D** none

_____ 2. In fact, she found both his book and his new pen.
- **A** book
- **B** book, pen
- **C** pen
- **D** none

_____ 3. They had been lying under Hank's desk all the time.
- **A** desk
- **B** They
- **C** Hank's
- **D** none

_____ 4. Ludwig van Beethoven composed nine symphonies and other works.
- **A** symphonies
- **B** symphonies, works
- **C** nine
- **D** none

_____ 5. Orchestras all over the world perform and record his music.
- **A** music
- **B** his
- **C** world
- **D** none

_____ 6. Philip thanked his father for all his help with the woodworking project.
- **A** father
- **B** help
- **C** project
- **D** none

_____ 7. The energetic students raced into the school yard before the bell.
- **A** students
- **B** yard, bell
- **C** bell
- **D** none

_____ 8. The meadowlark can sing fifty different songs.
- **A** fifty
- **B** different
- **C** songs
- **D** none

_____ 9. I ripped the wrapping paper off the box and slowly opened the lid.
- **A** paper
- **B** lid
- **C** paper, lid
- **D** none

_____ 10. Gorillas eat fruits and vegetables.
- **A** fruits, vegetables
- **B** fruits
- **C** vegetables
- **D** none

_____ 11. The contents of the box fell onto the floor.
- **A** box
- **B** contents
- **C** floor
- **D** none

_____ 12. Did you see her at the dance last night?
- **A** dance
- **B** her, dance
- **C** her
- **D** none

CHAPTER 16 Direct Objects

EXERCISE Underline the direct object(s) in each sentence.

1. A grapefruit tree can bear 1,500 pounds of fruit each year.

2. Nathan carried three boxes up the stairs.

3. Susan placed the clean sheets and pillowcases on the bed in the guest room.

4. Ecuador gets its name from the equator.

5. Have you ever had a parrot for a pet?

6. Joel cut the apple into quarters and then ate it.

7. Heat may damage the film in a camera.

8. We found five dollars on the path by the pond.

9. He bought two posters for his room and hung them up on the wall.

10. The flounder has both of its eyes on the right side of its body.

11. Robin drove her car slowly down the dark road.

12. Make your bed and clean your room.

CHAPTER 16 Indirect Objects

[16C.2] An **indirectobject** answers the questions *To* or *For whom*? or *To* or *For what*? after an action verb.

EXERCISE Write the indirect object(s) in each sentence.

_____ 1. Please send Grandmother a picture of yourself.

_____ 2. Did you lend Tony the old shovel or the new one?

_____ 3. The babysitter sang the baby and his brother a lullaby.

_____ 4. Todd gave the new student a helpful pamphlet about the school.

_____ 5. Will you lend me your umbrella?

_____ 6. Tad gave the fence a fresh coat of paint.

_____ 7. Mrs. Jenkins showed our class a film.

_____ 8. We loaned Tony and Maria our skis.

_____ 9. Show Sam the pictures of your trip to Alabama.

_____ 10. My sister sent him a card on his birthday.

_____ 11. Show me your new watch.

_____ 12. Apparently, a ghost gives guests a fright at that hotel.

_____ 13. Please leave me the schedules for the ferry to the island.

_____ 14. Ray and Steven both brought the party host bananas.

_____ 15. I gave Alexander the novel and Patsy the book of poems.

_____ 16. The volunteers served the children some hot vegetable soup.

_____ 17. Lisa Beth asked Cecilia two questions.

_____ 18. Please leave me three dollars on the counter for tomorrow's lunch.

_____ 19. Stephanie told Jeff the secret to her award-winning roses.

Name _____   Date _____

CHAPTER 16 Direct and Indirect Objects

EXERCISE Decide whether each underlined word is a direct object, an indirect object, or neither.

_____ 1. Wilbur Wright made his first famous <u>flight</u> in 1903.
  A direct object
  B indirect object
  C neither

_____ 2. His brother Orville had accompanied <u>him</u>.
  A direct object
  B indirect object
  C neither

_____ 3. Five years later he gave a <u>friend</u> a two-minute ride.
  A direct object
  B indirect object
  C neither

_____ 4. This friend became the first female <u>airplane</u> passenger.
  A direct object
  B indirect object
  C neither

_____ 5. Before takeoff from Auvers, France, Mrs. Hart O. Berg prepared <u>herself</u> and her clothing for the rough ride.
  A direct object
  B indirect object
  C neither

_____ 6. She tied her <u>hat</u> onto her head with a scarf.
  A direct object
  B indirect object
  C neither

_____ 7. With a cord she gathered her full <u>skirt</u> around her ankles.
  A direct object
  B indirect object
  C neither

_____ 8. As a result the wind would not blow her skirt or entangle it in the <u>controls</u>.
  A direct object
  B indirect object
  C neither

_____ 9. After the short flight, Mrs. Berg walked away from the <u>plane</u>.
  A direct object
  B indirect object
  C neither

_____ 10. She left the <u>scarf</u> on her hat and the cord on her skirt.
  A direct object
  B indirect object
  C neither

_____ 11. French observers admired her <u>idea</u> and adopted the new fashion.
  A direct object
  B indirect object
  C neither

_____ 12. Fashionable Frenchwomen sent their <u>dressmakers</u> new orders for such skirts.
  A direct object
  B indirect object
  C neither

_____ 13. Parisian designers embraced the new <u>style</u>.
  A direct object
  B indirect object
  C neither

_____ 14. Mrs. Berg had created the "hobble <u>skirt</u>."
  A direct object
  B indirect object
  C neither

CHAPTER 16 Finding Linking Verbs and Predicate Nominatives

[16C.3] A **predicatenominative** is a noun or a pronoun that follows a linking verb and identifies, renames, or explains the subject.

> **EXERCISE** Underline the linking verb and circle the predicate nominative in each sentence.

1. Ms. Nobles was my teacher for two years.

2. Mr. Lee is my coach this year.

3. Mark Twain was a popular writer who wrote many classics.

4. Samuel Clemens was his real name.

5. Leonard Bernstein was a fine pianist in his day.

6. He became a great conductor.

7. He was an excellent composer too.

8. Queenie is a tiny brown poodle who lives in the neighborhood.

9. She has always been a gentle dog compared to the others.

10. Marie Curie was a famous scientist.

11. Pierre Curie, also a scientist, was her husband.

12. He became a famous scientist too.

13. Radium was their major scientific discovery.

CHAPTER 16 Predicate Adjectives

[16C.4] A **predicateadjective** is an adjective that follows a linking verb and modifi es the subject.

EXERCISEA Identify the predicate adjective(s) in each sentence.

_____ 1. A funnel will always be conical in shape.
- **A** funnel
- **B** conical
- **C** shape
- **D** in shape

_____ 2. The ears and legs of a hare are relatively long.
- **A** ears
- **B** legs
- **C** long
- **D** relatively long

_____ 3. The city of Mecca in Saudi Arabia is holy to Muslims.
- **A** city
- **B** Mecca
- **C** Saudi Arabia
- **D** holy

_____ 4. Mrs. Keller seldom becomes irritated or angry with anyone.
- **A** irritated
- **B** angry
- **C** irritated, angry
- **D** anyone

_____ 5. Our basement remains cool and comfortable during the summer.
- **A** cool
- **B** cool, comfortable
- **C** comfortable
- **D** summer

EXERCISEB Write the predicate adjective(s) in each sentence.

_____ 6. The air smells sweet after a rainfall.

_____ 7. Leaving the campsite will be difficult after such a great hiking trip.

_____ 8. The players stayed energized because there were some college scouts at the game.

_____ 9. After a fresh coat of paint, our car appears new.

_____ 10. Hollyhocks grow high, reaching up to five feet sometimes.

_____ 11. Zeke, our dog, looked soft and fluffy after his bath.

_____ 12. Melanie is happy that it's not supposed to rain tomorrow.

CHAPTER 16   Subject Complements

> **EXERCISE** Decide if each underlined word is a predicate nominative, predicate adjective, or neither.

_____ 1. In 1953, Jacqueline Cochran became the first <u>woman</u> to break the speed of sound.

    A predicate nominative
    B predicate adjective
    C neither

_____ 2. Hirohito became <u>emperor</u> of Japan in 1926.

    A predicate nominative
    B predicate adjective
    C neither

_____ 3. An Oscar® is given for the best movie, but a Maggie is the <u>award</u> for the best magazine.

    A predicate nominative
    B predicate adjective
    C neither

_____ 4. A boysenberry bush may be <u>prickly</u>, but the berries are large and luscious.

    A predicate nominative
    B predicate adjective
    C neither

_____ 5. An English horn is quite similar to an oboe, but it is <u>larger</u> and sounds lower.

    A predicate nominative
    B predicate adjective
    C neither

_____ 6. The baby was crying earlier but seems <u>happy</u> now.

    A predicate nominative
    B predicate adjective
    C neither

_____ 7. Mesopotamia was an <u>ancient</u> country in the Middle East.

    A predicate nominative
    B predicate adjective
    C neither

_____ 8. Roodepoort-Maraisburg is a <u>city</u> of almost 100,000 people near Johannesburg, South Africa.

    A predicate nominative
    B predicate adjective
    C neither

_____ 9. A good spatula should be flexible and should have a broad and <u>flat</u> blade.

    A predicate nominative
    B predicate adjective
    C neither

_____ 10. Trolley cars might still be <u>useful</u>, but unfortunately they have become obsolete almost everywhere.

    A predicate nominative
    B predicate adjective
    C neither

CHAPTER 16   The Sentence Base Review

EXERCISE Write the letter of the term that correctly identifies the underlined word or words in the following paragraph.

(1) Read this message to learn about the most exciting product of the year! The Superbox is an amazing new (2) entertainment system. (3) The only entertainment system you'll ever need. (4) There are several reasons to buy this product. It plays (5) games, movies, and music on demand. With the Superbox, you (6) can read books, (draw) pictures, or (chat) with your friends. (7) Adults and children alike (8) can enjoy the Superbox. In fact, you can give (9) anyone the Superbox. They (10) are sure to love it. (11) What are you waiting for? (12) Buy a Superbox today!

_____ 1. **A** inverted order
   B predicate adjective
   C sentence fragment
   D understood subject

_____ 2. **A** complete subject
   B predicate nominative
   C compound verb
   D verb phrase

_____ 3. **A** inverted order
   B natural order
   C sentence fragment
   D compound subject

_____ 4. **A** inverted order
   B compound verb
   C predicate adjective
   D compound subject

_____ 5. **A** direct object
   B indirect object
   C predicate nominative
   D predicate adjective

_____ 6. **A** inverted order
   B compound verb
   C compound subject
   D predicate adjective

_____ 7. **A** inverted order
   B compound verb
   C compound subject
   D predicate adjective

_____ 8. **A** verb phrase
   B complete predicate
   C compound verb
   D simple subject

_____ 9. **A** direct object
   B indirect object
   C predicate nominative
   D predicate adjective

_____ 10. **A** simple subject
   B compound subject
   C simple predicate
   D complete predicate

_____ 11. **A** understood subject
   B predicate adjective
   C sentence fragment
   D inverted order

_____ 12. **A** complete subject
   B inverted order
   C understood subject
   D sentence fragment

CHAPTER 17 Adjectival Phrases

[17A] A **phrase** is a group of related words that functions as a single part of speech. A phrase does not have a subject and a verb.

[17A.1] An **adjectival phrase** is a prepositional phrase that is used to modify a noun or a pronoun.

EXERCISE A Choose the adjectival phrase in each sentence.

_____ 1. The gray cat on the welcome mat is sleeping.
   A gray cat
   B on the welcome mat
   C is sleeping

_____ 2. Chess is the name of the game store I work at.
   A Chess is the name
   B of the game store
   C I work at

_____ 3. The orange sweater in the closet is Kevin's.
   A orange
   B in the closet
   C is Kevin's

_____ 4. The sailors told tall tales about faraway places.
   A The sailors told
   B told tall tales
   C about faraway places

_____ 5. The film on the television was interrupted by a news brief.
   A on the television
   B was interrupted
   C by a news brief

_____ 6. The aorta is an essential part of the heart.
   A The aorta is
   B an essential part
   C of the heart

EXERCISE B Underline the adjectival phrase or phrases in each sentence.

7. In the Senate, sixteen is the minimum age for a page.

8. A frog in the swamp croaked loudly all night long.

9. That dish in the glass platter is not so tasty.

10. The dog in the kennel was happy to see his owners.

11. The radio in the kitchen doesn't work.

12. The last twenty minutes of the movie at Cinema I were dull.

13. None of the Pilgrims on the Mayflower had a middle name.

14. The captain of the debating team met the principal.

CHAPTER 17 Adverbial Phrases

[17A.2] An **adverbial phrase** is a prepositional phrase that is used to modify a verb, an adjective, or an adverb.

EXERCISE Underline the adverbial phrase or phrases in each sentence.

---

1. Stu and Amy will meet at the corner.

2. They will meet at noon.

3. Ken is travelling by train.

4. Mrs. Ricci drove to the soccer game.

5. She drove with great care.

6. She drove in the afternoon.

7. A cricket chirps with its legs.

8. The steep trail goes to the mountaintop.

9. Before dawn the storm began.

10. Into the tree crashed the boulder.

11. Hockey pucks are kept in a refrigerator before a game.

12. A blue whale may weigh 5,000 pounds at birth.

13. Since Wednesday we have been rehearsing the play.

14. The band performed on the field during halftime.

15. A small boy on the riverbank fished for trout.

16. During the winter a person cannot catch a cold at the North Pole.

17. I am very happy about your promotion.

18. A bird sees everything at once in total focus.

19. During the marathon we sat on the curbstone.

20. Some lizards can run on their hind legs.

CHAPTER 17 Adjectival and Adverbial Phrases

EXERCISE Decide whether each underlined prepositional phrase is used as an adjectival phrase or an adverbial phrase.

_____ 1. The true king <u>of the beasts</u> is the elephant.

    A adjectival phrase
    B adverbial phrase

_____ 2. The elephant rules <u>with complete ease</u> in its kingdom.

    A adjectival phrase
    B adverbial phrase

_____ 3. Most creatures can, however, venture <u>near an elephant</u> without fear.

    A adjectival phrase
    B adverbial phrase

_____ 4. An elephant is instantly recognizable <u>because of its size</u> and because of its trunk.

    A adjectival phrase
    B adverbial phrase

_____ 5. With its trunk an elephant can uproot a tree <u>with relative ease</u>.

    A adjectival phrase
    B adverbial phrase

_____ 6. With the same trunk, an elephant can lift a tiny peanut <u>from the ground</u>.

    A adjectival phrase
    B adverbial phrase

_____ 7. The elephant also smells, drinks, feeds itself, and even gives itself a shower, all <u>with its trunk</u>.

    A adjectival phrase
    B adverbial phrase

_____ 8. Furthermore, the sensitive tip <u>of its trunk</u> can detect the shape, texture, and temperature of an object.

    A adjectival phrase
    B adverbial phrase

_____ 9. <u>With its trunk</u> an elephant gives an affectionate caress to its baby or its mate.

    A adjectival phrase
    B adverbial phrase

_____ 10. Against an enemy, however, it is used <u>as a weapon</u>.

    A adjectival phrase
    B adverbial phrase

_____ 11. In my opinion, the trunk is the most amazing part <u>of this amazing animal</u>.

    A adjectival phrase
    B adverbial phrase

Date

Appositives and Appositive Phrases

[17B] An **appositive** is a noun or a pronoun that identifies or explains another noun or pronoun in the sentence.

[17B.1] An appositive with modifiers is called an **appositive phrase**.

EXERCISE A Select the noun that the underlined appositive or appositive phrase modifies.

_____ 1. My friend <u>Jason</u> eats yogurt with raisins every day.
A friend
B yogurt
C raisins
D day

_____ 2. The poet <u>Emily Dickinson</u> spent all her life in the same house.
A poet
B spent
C life
D house

_____ 3. Elizabeth, <u>the Queen of England</u>, has four children.
A Elizabeth
B has
C four
D children

_____ 4. I met Mrs. Kolba, <u>my English teacher</u>, on the way to school.
A I
B Mrs. Kolba
C way
D school

_____ 5. Francis liked his birthday present, <u>a pair of ice skates</u>.
A Francis
B birthday
C present
D skates

_____ 6. Cockroaches, <u>those troublesome insects</u>, are found all over the world.
A Cockroaches
B insects
C found
D world

EXERCISE B Underline each appositive or appositive phrase in the sentences below. Then circle the noun that the underlined appositive or appositive phrase modifies.

7. Denver, the capital of Colorado, is also its largest city.

8. The phone call was from Marshall, my sister's friend.

9. A good basketball player, Carla practices every day.

10. I read two stories by the writer Ray Bradbury this week.

11. Samantha, my cousin, made me this beaded necklace.

12. His sister, the one in the blue sweatshirt, plays in a band.

CHAPTER 17 **Combining Sentences Using Appositive Phrases**

EXERCISE A Choose the answer that correctly combines the pair of sentences with an appositive.

_____ 1. The German composer was also a pianist. The composer was Brahms.
  A The German composer was also a pianist; the composer was Brahms.
  B The German composer and pianist was Brahms.
  C The German composer Brahms was also a pianist.

_____ 2. Prague is the capital of the Czech Republic. It has more than a million people.
  A Prague is the capital of the Czech Republic; it has over a million people.
  B The capital of the Czech Republic, Prague, has over a million people.
  C The capital of the Czech Republic, which has over a million people, is Prague.

_____ 3. The game is named after a sixteenth-century Italian painter. The game is Botticelli.
  A Botticelli is the game named after a sixteenth-century Italian painter.
  B The game Botticelli is named after a sixteenth-century Italian painter.
  C The game of Botticelli is named after a sixteenth-century Italian painter.

EXERCISE B Combine each pair of sentences using an appositive.

4. Sears and Roebuck is a large chain of retail stores in the United States. It was actually founded by Mr. Sears and Mr. Roebuck.

_____

_____

_____

5. Judy Garland sang "Over the Rainbow" more than 12,000 times. It is a song from *The Wizard of Oz.*

_____

_____

_____

6. The Green Revolution was a series of changes in farming methods. It was led by Norman Borlaug.

_____

_____

_____

continued

Chapter 17: Combining Sentences Using Appositive Phrases *continued*

7. Henry is going to compete in the statewide track meet. He has been my best friend since first grade.

_____

_____

_____

8. *Sabrina* is a love story starring Audrey Hepburn, Humphrey Bogart, and William Holden. It is my favorite movie.

_____

_____

_____

Name _____   Date _____

Finding Participles and Participial Phrases

[17C.1] A **participle** is a verb form that is used as an adjective.

[17C.3] A **participial phrase** is a participle with its modifiers and complements—all working together as an adjective.

EXERCISE Choose the participle or participial phrase modifying the underlined noun in each sentence.

_____ 1. Mr. Jones spoke to the waiting <u>students</u>.

    A Mr. Jones
    B spoke
    C to the waiting
    D waiting

_____ 2. He will speak to the <u>students</u> waiting outside.

    A He
    B will speak
    C waiting outside
    D outside

_____ 3. The <u>students</u>, waiting for a test, sit quietly.

    A waiting
    B waiting for a test
    C sit quietly
    D quietly

_____ 4. Their planned <u>trip</u> to Maine begins tomorrow.

    A Their
    B planned
    C Maine
    D tomorrow

_____ 5. Planned by Mrs. Harris, the <u>trip</u> was a success.

    A Planned by Mrs. Harris
    B Mrs. Harris
    C was
    D a success

_____ 6. We must cancel the <u>trip</u> planned for today.

    A We
    B must cancel
    C planned for today
    D today

_____ 7. The <u>girl</u> waving at us is my cousin.

    A waving at us
    B at us
    C my
    D cousin

_____ 8. On the way you will pass a <u>house</u> painted yellow.

    A On the way
    B pass
    C painted yellow
    D yellow

_____ 9. <u>Grant</u>, blinded by the sun, missed the ball.

    A blinded by the sun
    B sun
    C missed the ball
    D ball

_____ 10. Walking to school, <u>Daisy</u> planned her afternoon activities.

    A Walking to school
    B school
    C planned her afternoon activities
    D activities

_____ 11. No one answered the ringing <u>doorbell</u>.

    A answered
    B ringing
    C No one answered
    D answered the ringing

_____ 12. <u>James Zaharee</u>, using a fine pen and a microscope, printed the Gettysburg Address on a human hair.

    A using
    B printed
    C using a fine pen and a microscope
    D printed the Gettysburg Address

CHAPTER 17   Finding Participles and Participial Phrases

EXERCISE Circle the participle or participial phrase modifying the underlined noun in each sentence.

1. The flag of Denmark is the oldest unchanged national <u>flag</u> in existence.

2. The <u>meeting</u>, annoying and disorganized, was a waste of time.

3. The largest jigsaw <u>puzzle</u>, made in 1954, contained more than 10,000 pieces.

4. One of the oldest <u>games</u>, played since prehistoric times, is marbles.

5. The redwoods are the tallest living <u>things</u> on our planet.

6. Living off the coast of Japan, the largest <u>crabs</u> in the world stand three feet high and weigh thirty pounds.

7. The speeding <u>car</u> almost crashed.

8. <u>Bloodhounds</u>, often used in detective work, can detect a ten-day-old scent.

9. Swimming rapidly, <u>John Sigmund</u> traveled 292 miles down the Mississippi River in 90 hours.

10. Please empty the overflowing <u>trash</u>.

11. The <u>hikers</u>, hungry and exhausted, returned to their base camp.

12. The barking <u>dog</u> kept me awake all night.

13. The smallest bird is the <u>bee hummingbird</u>, measuring only two-and-a-half inches.

14. Don't step on the broken <u>glass</u> on the floor.

15. Those <u>nails</u>, rusted and bent, are a hazard.

16. In Ohio someone found an eagle's <u>nest</u> weighing two tons.

17. A talking <u>doll</u> was one of Thomas Edison's many clever inventions.

18. The highest wind <u>velocity</u> recorded in the United States was 231 miles per hour.

19. Oranges and cantaloupes are <u>fruits</u> containing vitamin C.

20. Our reserved <u>seats</u> were located beside a window.

21. We watched the <u>chickadees</u> fluttering around the bird feeder.

CHAPTER 17 Finding Gerunds and Gerund Phrases

[17C.4] A **gerund** is a verb form that is used as a noun.

[17C.5] A **gerund phrase** is a gerund with its modifiers and complements—all working together as a noun.

EXERCISE Underline the complete gerund or gerund phrase in each sentence.

1. Cheering the team gave me a sore throat.

2. My uncle is taking up a new kind of exercise, walking.

3. Juana's mother enjoys preserving fruits and vegetables.

4. Arriving early was the right thing to do.

5. The puppy's soft whining was coming from under the stairs.

6. Swimming is one of the best forms of exercise.

7. Galileo made his first telescope by placing a lens at each end of an organ pipe.

8. She has just finished a course in typing.

9. Please stop that yelling!

10. Sinking 499 free throws in a row is Ellen's present claim to fame.

11. An early method of food preservation was pickling.

12. A snail can cross the edge of the sharpest razor without cutting itself.

13. The ancient Egyptians avoided killing any sacred animal.

14. The hungry boys gave eating their full attention.

15. That rude couple's whispering bothered everyone in the audience.

16. Josh's plan, rushing the passer, seemed sound to us.

17. Kingfishers build nests by tunneling into the sides of riverbanks.

18. Lee has a new hobby, painting.

19. I appreciate your helping me with my homework.

20. A common experience for everyone is dreaming.

CHAPTER 17 ## Distinguishing Between Infinitives and Prepositional Phrases

[17C.6] An **infinitive** is a verb form that usually begins with *to*. It is used as a noun, an adjective, or an adverb.

EXERCISE Write I if the underlined group of words is an infinitive or P if it is a prepositional phrase.

_____ 1. Han hurried <u>to dress</u>.

_____ 2. He hurried <u>to school</u>.

_____ 3. His class was going <u>to the mint</u>.

_____ 4. He needed <u>to arrive</u> early.

_____ 5. He wanted <u>to stop</u> at the library.

_____ 6. He went there <u>to return</u> a book.

_____ 7. He handed it <u>to the librarian</u>.

_____ 8. He had read it <u>to learn</u> about coins.

_____ 9. He planned <u>to write</u> a report about money.

_____ 10. <u>To visit</u> the mint would be useful.

_____ 11. Will you please bring these books <u>to Jenni</u>?

_____ 12. Now I would like <u>to speak</u>.

_____ 13. Should we take the dog <u>to Tennessee</u> with us?

_____ 14. Jeff just learned <u>to ski</u>.

_____ 15. That stereo is too expensive <u>to buy</u>.

_____ 16. What do you want <u>to say</u>?

_____ 17. Zach said he will give me a ride <u>to work</u>.

_____ 18. The oboe is the hardest woodwind <u>to master</u>.

_____ 19. The best way <u>to go</u> would be Route 62.

_____ 20. Let's go out <u>to dinner</u> this weekend.

CHAPTER 17 Distinguishing Between Infinitives and Prepositional Phrases

EXERCISE Underline each infinitive or prepositional phrase. Then choose whether the underlined group of words is an infinitive or a prepositional phrase.

_____ 1. Your teacher will give you the topic to research.
   A infinitive
   B prepositional phrase

_____ 2. Let's walk to school today.
   A infinitive
   B prepositional phrase

_____ 3. I need some time to rest.
   A infinitive
   B prepositional phrase

_____ 4. Take this playbook to Coach.
   A infinitive
   B prepositional phrase

_____ 5. To relax is difficult for some people.
   A infinitive
   B prepositional phrase

_____ 6. I'll go to church with you.
   A infinitive
   B prepositional phrase

_____ 7. Give that message to Larry.
   A infinitive
   B prepositional phrase

_____ 8. The items to sell are on the table.
   A infinitive
   B prepositional phrase

_____ 9. I will try to define the word for you.
   A infinitive
   B prepositional phrase

_____ 10. The crossword puzzle is easy to do.
   A infinitive
   B prepositional phrase

_____ 11. The shoe was marketed to athletes.
   A infinitive
   B prepositional phrase

_____ 12. To understand these formulas is my goal.
   A infinitive
   B prepositional phrase

_____ 13. Take this pencil to class with you.
   A infinitive
   B prepositional phrase

_____ 14. Mia is planning to return.
   A infinitive
   B prepositional phrase

_____ 15. Their words were too muffled to understand.
   A infinitive
   B prepositional phrase

CHAPTER 17 Misplaced Modifiers

[17A.3] When a phrase is too far away from the word it modifies, the result may be a **misplaced modifier**.

EXERCISE Write M if the sentence contains a misplaced modifier or C if the sentence is correctly written.

_____ 1. Hiding under a rock, I saw a lizard.

_____ 2. Swollen because of the rain, we feared the raging river.

_____ 3. Hiking down the trail, Michiko spotted a brown bear.

_____ 4. Chattering angrily in the bushes, we heard a squirrel.

_____ 5. Walking to school, Gary saw two stalled automobiles.

_____ 6. Shoveling the sidewalk, Trudy found a bracelet.

_____ 7. Carmen saw the school bus looking out the window.

_____ 8. Pecking holes in the tree, Jack saw a woodpecker.

_____ 9. Hopping through the woods, I saw the rabbit.

_____ 10. Earl found an old cabin walking in the woods.

_____ 11. Reading *Wildlife* magazine, Ned examined a picture of a rhinoceros.

_____ 12. Lynn dropped the letter in the mailbox glancing at her watch.

_____ 13. Studying the map, I found the town.

_____ 14. We saw a glove frozen to the pavement.

_____ 15. Roger noticed a raccoon riding down the dirt road.

CHAPTER 17 Misplaced and Dangling Modifiers

[17C.8] When participial and infinitive phrases are placed too far from the word they modify, they become **misplaced modifiers**.

[17C.9] A verbal phrase that has nothing to describe is called a **dangling modifier**.

EXERCISE Decide whether each sentence is correctly written or whether it contains a misplaced or dangling modifier.

_____ 1. Licking its whiskers, Tammy observed a small tabby cat.

    A misplaced modifier
    B correct

_____ 2. The jockey rode the horse wearing a bright purple jockey's uniform and the number 15.

    A misplaced modifier
    B correct

_____ 3. To dine at our table, a guest must first wash his or her hands.

    A dangling modifier
    B correct

_____ 4. Lacking a proper heating system, the couple moved into their new home.

    A misplaced modifier
    B correct

_____ 5. Hanging on the museum wall, Hank observed many colorful paintings.

    A misplaced modifier
    B correct

_____ 6. Made with sugar, flour, and water, the little girl presented us with her cookies.

    A misplaced modifier
    B correct

_____ 7. To try out for the team, the roster must first be signed.

    A dangling modifier
    B correct

_____ 8. To withdraw money, one should first type a secret password.

    A dangling modifier
    B correct

_____ 9. Strolling down the path, the boy witnessed a flock of geese.

    A misplaced modifier
    B correct

_____ 10. To interest the team in winning, pictures of the other team members were placed on the blackboard.

    A dangling modifier
    B correct

_____ 11. To win the race, the finish line must be in sight.

    A dangling modifier
    B correct

_____ 12. Singing his favorite song, Marvin smiled and looked into the mirror.

    A misplaced modifier
    B correct

_____ 13. Looking for the missing keys, the suggestion was made to stop and concentrate for a moment.

    A dangling modifier
    B correct

_____ 14. To find your way to my house, you must cross many busy streets.

    A dangling modifier
    B correct

continued

Chapter 17: Misplaced and Dangling Modifiers *continued*

_____ 15. There is Dan's glove on the home team's bench with the red stitching on its fingers.

    A misplaced modifier

    B correct

_____ 16. To win my attention, many gifts must be bought.

    A dangling modifier

    B correct

_____ 17. We watched the two squirrels searching for chestnuts.

    A misplaced modifier

    B correct

CHAPTER 17 Correcting Misplaced and Dangling Modifiers

EXERCISE Rewrite each sentence to correct a misplaced or dangling modifier.

1. I dropped my books in the mud sprinting for the bus.

   _____

   _____

2. To show what you have learned so far, extreme care should be taken.

   _____

   _____

3. Riding in heavy traffic, the noise was deafening.

   _____

   _____

4. The little girls began to cook their mud pies laughing with glee.

   _____

   _____

5. We saw a hummingbird strolling through the flowers.

   _____

   _____

6. Running from place to place, it was a very busy day.

   _____

   _____

7. To do a crossword puzzle, a dictionary is handy.

   _____

   _____

8. Screeching in pain, the needle was removed from her hand.

   _____

   _____

continued

Chapter 17: Correcting Misplaced and Dangling Modifiers *continued*

9. Bowing before the audience, the applause began to echo through Simpson's ears.

_____

_____

10. Wishing to be a part-time clerk, the ad caught my eye.

_____

_____

Name _____ Date _____

CHAPTER 17 Correcting Misplaced and Dangling Modifiers

EXERCISE A Each item contains a sentence written three different ways. Choose the sentence in which NO misplaced modifier blurs the meaning of the sentence and makes it incorrect.

_____ 1. **A** Trudy was looking for a story about kangaroos in the library.
B Trudy was looking for a story in the library about kangaroos.
C Trudy was looking in the library for a story about kangaroos.

_____ 2. **A** The outfielder fell on his back and caught the ball.
B The outfielder fell and caught the ball on his back.
C The outfielder on his back fell and caught the ball.

_____ 3. **A** Mrs. Benjamin spoke to us about the two world wars on Friday.
B About the two world wars on Friday, Mrs. Benjamin spoke to us.
C On Friday Mrs. Benjamin spoke to us about the two world wars.

_____ 4. **A** They could see most of New York City on top of the tallest building.
B From the top of the tallest building, they could see most of New York City.
C They could see on the top of the tallest buildings most of New York City.

_____ 5. **A** The old man was chasing the dog with a cane.
B With a cane the dog was chased by the old man.
C The old man with a cane was chasing the dog.

EXERCISE B Select the answer that corrects each sentence containing a misplaced or dangling modifier. If the sentence is correct, choose D.

_____ 6. To go to the library, takes the Riverside bus.
A To go to the library, she takes the Riverside bus.
B Takes the Riverside bus, to go to the library.
C To go to the library, it takes the Riverside bus.
D No change

_____ 7. A baby wrapped in blankets is in the carriage.
A Wrapped in blankets, a carriage contains a baby.
B In the carriage wrapped in blankets is a baby.
C A baby is in the carriage wrapped in blankets.
D No change

_____ 8. Washing his car, a cat watched Mr. Ruiz.
A A cat washing his car watched Mr. Ruiz.
B A cat, washing his car, watched Mr. Ruiz.
C A cat watched Mr. Ruiz washing his car.
D No change

_____ 9. To receive a prize, a ticket stub must be shown.
A A ticket stub, to receive a prize, must be shown.
B To receive a prize, you must show a ticket stub.
C A ticket stub must be shown receiving a prize.
D No change

Name _____ Date _____

CHAPTER 17 Phrases Review

EXERCISE Write the letter of the term that correctly identifies the underlined phrase in each sentence.

A cruise ship is a passenger vessel **(1)** <u>featuring many of the attractions of a luxury resort</u>. For many years **(2)** <u>vacationing on a cruise ship</u> has been a popular activity. **(3)** <u>To entertain passengers</u>, a cruise ship may house restaurants, nightclubs, swimming pools, spas, and more. The first ship to be built **(4)** <u>for this purpose</u> was launched in 1900. This vessel, **(5)** <u>the *Prinzessin Victoria Luise*</u>, held just 120 cabins. **(6)** <u>By comparison</u>, the largest cruise ship **(7)** <u>on the seas today</u> carries more than 3,600 passengers and 1,300 crew. **(8)** <u>In 1906</u>, the captain of the *Victoria Luise*, **(9)** <u>misjudging the distance from shore</u>, crashed the ship into rocks. But despite its short career, the *Victoria Luise* began a thriving industry that millions **(10)** <u>of people</u> have enjoyed.

_____ 1. **A** participial phrase
B gerund phrase
C infinitive phrase
D adverbial phrase

_____ 2. **A** participial phrase
B gerund phrase
C infinitive phrase
D appositive phrase

_____ 3. **A** gerund phrase
B infinitive phrase
C participial phrase
D prepositional phrase

_____ 4. **A** adjectival phrase
B appositive phrase
C infinitive phrase
D adverbial phrase

_____ 5. **A** adjectival phrase
B adverbial phrase
C appositive phrase
D gerund phrase

_____ 6. **A** adjectival phrase
B adverbial phrase
C appositive phrase
D participial phrase

_____ 7. **A** adjectival phrase
B adverbial phrase
C appositive phrase
D gerund phrase

_____ 8. **A** infinitive phrase
B appositive phrase
C adverbial phrase
D adjectival phrase

_____ 9. **A** prepositional phrase
B participial phrase
C appositive phrase
D gerund phrase

_____ 10. **A** appositive phrase
B adverbial phrase
C infinitive phrase
D adjectival phrase

CHAPTER 18 Independent and Subordinate Clauses

[18A] A **clause** is a group of words that is part of a sentence and has a subject and a verb.

[18A.1] An **independent (main) clause** can stand alone as a sentence because it expresses a complete thought.

[18A.2] A **subordinate (dependent) clause** cannot stand alone as a sentence because it does not express a complete thought.

EXERCISE A Write I if the underlined clause is independent or S if it is subordinate.

_____ 1. Mrs. Santos sat in the chair that was by the window.

_____ 2. Mrs. Santos sat in the chair, and Maggie sat on the floor.

_____ 3. Mrs. Santos sat in the chair as she talked to Maggie.

_____ 4. After dinner, the telephone rang.

_____ 5. If the telephone rings, Luke will answer it.

_____ 6. The telephone rang, and Luke answered it.

_____ 7. The telephone rang before Luke left the house.

_____ 8. Alma locks the door when she goes out.

_____ 9. The day was cool, but the summer wasn't over yet.

_____ 10. Before the sun set, we went for a swim.

EXERCISE B Underline each independent clause.

11. Woodrow Wilson, who was our twenty-eighth president, was a Democrat.

12. As you may know, the vice president that Wilson chose was named Thomas R. Marshall.

13. Before lunch, we learned about presidents in history class.

14. I enjoy history, a class that Mr. Preston teaches.

15. Mr. Preston knows a lot about politics, and he makes us eager to learn.

16. Since I'm interested in American history, he has prompted me to do a report about Woodrow Wilson.

17. I have learned many things, including this fact: Wilson was once governor of New Jersey.

CHAPTER 18 Adverbial Clauses

[18B.1] An **adverbial clause** is a subordinate clause that is used like an adverb to modify a verb, an adjective, or an adverb.

EXERCISE A Choose the complete adverbial clause in each sentence.

_____ 1. When the curtain falls, the audience applauds.
  A When the curtain falls
  B the audience applauds

_____ 2. If the telephone rings, Paul will answer it.
  A If the telephone rings
  B Paul will answer it

_____ 3. That dish has been cracked since Lillian dropped it.
  A That dish has been cracked
  B since Lillian dropped it

_____ 4. Wilbur listened to the radio while he folded the laundry.
  A to the radio
  B while he folded the laundry

_____ 5. The dress will fit Becky as long as she doesn't grow.
  A will fit Becky
  B as long as she doesn't grow

_____ 6. Before clocks were invented, various devices were used to tell time.
  A Before clocks were invented
  B used to tell time

EXERCISE B Underline the complete adverbial clause in each sentence.

7. Sundials were effective as long as the sun was shining.

8. Ropes tied in regularly spaced knots measured time as they burned.

9. When all the sand had trickled through the narrow midsection of an hourglass, an hour had passed.

10. Convenient and accurate timekeeping did not exist until clocks came into use in the 1700s.

11. United States Marines are called leathernecks because their coats once had big leather collars.

12. A tornado once sheared a whole herd of sheep while they grazed.

13. I will exercise as long as you do.

14. Although Columbus made four voyages to the Americas, he never discovered the coast of the mainland.

CHAPTER 18 Adverbial Clauses

EXERCISE A Choose the word or words that the adverbial clause modifies in each sentence.

_____ 1. Meet me in the library before class starts.
  A Meet
  B starts

_____ 2. As far as I know, Suki fed the dog.
  A dog
  B know

_____ 3. When one cup of rice is cooked, it expands to three.
  A is cooked
  B expands

_____ 4. I can type faster than anyone I know.
  A can type
  B faster

_____ 5. If you could jump like a grasshopper, you could leap over a house!
  A could leap
  B could jump

_____ 6. Unless I set the alarm, I will sleep until nine o'clock and be late for school.
  A set
  B will sleep

EXERCISE B Underline the adverbial clause in each sentence. Then circle the word or words that the adverbial clause modifies.

7. The Battle of New Orleans was fought after the peace treaty had been signed.

8. As Mother drove, Father studied the road map.

10. We can attend the meeting even though we aren't members.

11. They acted as if nothing had happened.

12. Whenever you are ready to go, just tell me.

13. Since cowbirds don't build nests, they lay their eggs in the nests of other birds.

14. This week is colder than the last two weeks have been.

15. I can't leave until I do my homework.

CHAPTER 18 Adjectival Clauses and Relative Pronouns

[18B.3] An **adjectival clause** is a subordinate clause that is used like an adjective to modify a noun or a pronoun.

[18B.4] A **relative pronoun** relates an adjectival clause to its antecedent—the noun or pronoun it modifies.

> **EXERCISE** Underline the adjectival clause in each sentence.

1. My mother and I are going to the sale that the antiques store is having.

2. This is the catalog that came in the mail last week.

3. The numbers that are written in red show the sale prices.

4. Mrs. Harper, who lives next door, will come with us.

5. That chair is the piece of furniture that she wants.

6. Unlike the organ, which dates back to Roman times, the piano is fairly modern.

7. Cristofori, who built the first piano, lived in Italy in the early eighteenth century.

8. Then German craftsmen, for whom every musical instrument was a challenge, improved its design.

9. By the 1770s, the piano had become the instrument that every European wanted.

10. It was the rare upper-class family whose household did not include a piano.

11. Would the student whose books were stolen please come to the office?

12. Alison, who did not want to go, actually wound up having fun.

13. The Mayflower Compact, which was signed in 1620, is interesting to read.

14. The health of the pug puppy we found is improving nicely.

15. The dresser, which we bought at the auction, is made of mahogany.

CHAPTER 18 Adjectival Clauses and Relative Pronouns

EXERCISE Decide the function of each relative pronoun (some are understood) in the underlined adjectival clause in each sentence.

_____ 1. The Carters, <u>whose dog I walk</u>, will be away for three weeks.

    A subject
    B direct object
    C object of a preposition
    D possessive

_____ 2. Lions <u>that are raised in captivity</u> are surprisingly tame.

    A subject
    B direct object
    C object of a preposition
    D possessive

_____ 3. Are you wearing the coat <u>you bought last week at the mall</u>?

    A subject
    B direct object
    C object of a preposition
    D possessive

_____ 4. The longest tunnel through <u>which we drove</u> was about a mile long.

    A subject
    B direct object
    C object of a preposition
    D possessive

_____ 5. Daniel Webster, <u>who became famous for his work in law</u>, never went to law school.

    A subject
    B direct object
    C object of a preposition
    D possessive

_____ 6. The records <u>I gave him</u> dated back to the 1950s.

    A subject
    B direct object
    C object of a preposition
    D possessive

_____ 7. The story, <u>whose author was unknown</u>, was comical.

    A subject
    B direct object
    C object of a preposition
    D possessive

_____ 8. A rat can gnaw through concrete <u>that is two feet thick</u>.

    A subject
    B direct object
    C object of a preposition
    D possessive

_____ 9. He is the man to <u>whom you must speak</u>.

    A subject
    B direct object
    C object of a preposition
    D possessive

_____ 10. The ostrich, <u>which is the largest of all birds</u>, can outrun a horse.

    A subject
    B direct object
    C object of a preposition
    D possessive

CHAPTER 18 — Misplaced Modifiers

[18B.7] A clause that is too far away from the word it modifies is called a **misplaced modifier**.

EXERCISE A Choose the word that the misplaced modifier should modify.

_____ 1. The birds ignored the dog that chirped in the trees.

    A dog
    B trees
    C that
    D birds

_____ 2. The present is on the table that I received for my birthday.

    A table
    B present
    C I
    D birthday

_____ 3. The ten-speed bicycle is in the garage that my father bought for me.

    A garage
    B father
    C bicycle
    D that

_____ 4. The movie will be shown in the auditorium which has Antarctica as the setting.

    A movie
    B Antarctica
    C auditorium
    D setting

_____ 5. Glenn repaired my car who's a good friend of mine.

    A Glenn
    B car
    C friend
    D mine

_____ 6. We met Mrs. Walker in the park who lives nearby.

    A park
    B We
    C Mrs. Walker
    D who

EXERCISE B Underline the word that the misplaced modifier should modify.

7. The note was a reminder to order Pat's birthday cake that was written on the calendar.

8. The CD is in the cabinet that I thought I had lost.

9. The rain flooded our basement which lasted a week.

10. The oak tree provides us with shade that grows in our backyard.

11. The teenager that the band had released bought the most recent CD.

12. The students did not have to take the final exam whose average was an A.

CHAPTER 18 Misplaced Modifiers

EXERCISE Rewrite each sentence to correct the misplaced modifier.

1. The horse should be placed in the stall whose leg is injured.

   _____

2. The leaves should be raked by Brittany that have fallen.

   _____

3. The friends were staying for the weekend to whom I served the meal.

   _____

4. The fish should not be served to the diner that smells spoiled.

   _____

5. This list of birth dates was requested by Dr. Neal, which is in chronological order.

   _____

6. Contestants will make it to the final round who answer this question correctly.

   _____

7. The date is incorrect that is written on the chalkboard.

   _____

8. My promises are as good as gold, which I never break.

   _____

9. The streets should be sprinkled with salt that are iced over.

   _____

10. The fax machine is in the corner, which is not for personal use.

    _____

11. This dessert is for Tanya, which is a fudge sundae.

    _____

12. The vines should be cut down that have climbed up the fence.

    _____

CHAPTER 18 Noun Clauses

[18B.8] A **noun clause** is a subordinate clause that is used like a noun.

EXERCISE Choose the noun clause for each sentence. Some sentences may contain more than one noun clause.

_____ 1. I can remember when I first met Pat, even though it was a long time ago.

   A when I first met Pat
   B a long time ago

_____ 2. We will take a vote and do whatever the majority wants.

   A take a vote
   B whatever the majority wants

_____ 3. When the mayor started speaking, no one in the back row could hear what he said.

   A When the mayor started speaking
   B what he said

_____ 4. The jury has to decide whose testimony they believe.

   A The jury has to decide
   B whose testimony they believe

_____ 5. How a tire is changed is an important thing for every driver to know.

   A How a tire is changed
   B for every driver to know

_____ 6. The eruptions of volcanoes are what Dr. Sweeney is studying.

   A The eruptions of volcanoes
   B what Dr. Sweeney is studying

_____ 7. Offer whomever attends the meeting a bumper sticker.

   A Offer whomever
   B whomever attends the meeting

_____ 8. The meteorologist explained how tornadoes are formed.

   A The meteorologist
   B how tornadoes are formed

_____ 9. That trees require huge quantities of water does not surprise me.

   A That trees require huge quantities of water
   B does not surprise me

_____ 10. Sylvester was unclear about when the science report was due.

   A Sylvester was unclear
   B when the science report was due

_____ 11. That Miriam deserved the prize for the best costume was not disputed by anyone.

   A That Miriam deserved the prize for the best costume
   B by anyone

_____ 12. I don't know what you mean.

   A I don't know
   B what you mean

CHAPTER 18 Noun Clauses

EXERCISE Underline the noun clause in each each sentence. Some sentences may contain more than one noun clause.

1. Are you really concerned with what is best for me?

2. What you say is true up to a point.

3. Some botanists believe that cabbage is the most ancient vegetable still grown today.

4. Does Pilar know where she stored the decorations?

5. The parrot speaks to whomever comes into the house.

6. Why the group had gathered at the mall was unknown.

7. Some people believe that snake meat is healthful.

8. The police always give a ticket to whomever parks in front of a hydrant.

9. For many years no one knew where tuna spawned.

10. We will go along with whatever you decide.

11. Give whomever calls the directions to our house.

12. I don't know why I said that.

13. How Jerry lost my bicycle is a big mystery.

CHAPTER 18 · Identifying Adverbial, Adjectival, and Noun Clauses

EXERCISE Underline the subordinate clause, if any, in each of the following sentences. Then identify each clause as an adverbial, adjectival, or noun clause. Choose *none* if the sentence has no subordinate clause.

_____ 1. Do you know what a Turkish bath is?

   A adverbial clause
   B adjectival clause
   C noun clause
   D none

_____ 2. Turkish soldiers spread the custom of hot-air baths in the Middle Ages.

   A adverbial clause
   B adjectival clause
   C noun clause
   D none

_____ 3. This is how you would take a Turkish bath today.

   A adverbial clause
   B adjectival clause
   C noun clause
   D none

_____ 4. First you enter a sweating room that has dry heat at a temperature of about 160°F (71°C).

   A adverbial clause
   B adjectival clause
   C noun clause
   D none

_____ 5. After that you proceed to a room filled with steam.

   A adverbial clause
   B adjectival clause
   C noun clause
   D none

_____ 6. After you have perspired freely, you wash thoroughly with soap.

   A adverbial clause
   B adjectival clause
   C noun clause
   D none

_____ 7. You may have your muscles massaged before you dry yourself with a rough towel.

   A adverbial clause
   B adjectival clause
   C noun clause
   D none

_____ 8. Anyone who considers this the end of the experience is wrong.

   A adverbial clause
   B adjectival clause
   C noun clause
   D none

_____ 9. You must next take a cold shower, which refreshes your body.

   A adverbial clause
   B adjectival clause
   C noun clause
   D none

_____ 10. Finally, you rest until your body temperature returns to normal.

   A adverbial clause
   B adjectival clause
   C noun clause
   D none

CHAPTER 18 Sentence Structure

[18C.1] A **simple sentence** consists of one independent clause.

[18C.2] A **compound sentence** consists of two or more independent clauses.

[18C.3] A **complex sentence** consists of one independent clause and one or more subordinate clauses.

EXERCISE Label each sentence as simple, compound, or complex.

_____ 1. Celia cut her finger.

_____ 2. Celia cut her finger, and Eric put a bandage on it.

_____ 3. Celia cut her finger as she was making the salad.

_____ 4. Simon changed the tire.

_____ 5. Tracy changed the tire, and Simon watched.

_____ 6. Simon changed the tire while Tracy watched.

_____ 7. Whenever Dad changed a tire, he watched.

_____ 8. His bicycle tire is flat, but he will fix it today.

_____ 9. Because his bicycle tire is flat, he cannot ride to the store.

_____ 10. His bicycle tire has been flat since he rode over a nail.

_____ 11. Mrs. Santos sat in the chair.

_____ 12. Mrs. Santos sat in the chair, and Maggie sat on the floor.

_____ 13. Mrs. Santos sat in the chair as she talked to Maggie.

_____ 14. The telephone rang.

_____ 15. If the telephone rings, Luke will answer it.

_____ 16. The telephone rang, and Luke answered it.

_____ 17. The telephone rang after Luke left the house.

_____ 18. Alma locks the door when she goes out.

_____ 19. The day was cool, but the summer wasn't over yet.

_____ 20. Before the sun set, we went for a swim.

CHAPTER 18 **Sentence Structure**

[18C.4] A **compound-complex** sentence consists of two or more independent clauses and one or more subordinate clauses.

EXERCISE Decide whether each sentence in the paragraph below is simple, compound, complex, or compound-complex.

(1) The great composer Ludwig van Beethoven changed the piano and piano-playing forever. (2) When pianos first became popular, they were seen as delicate instruments. (3) Pianists played with a light touch and produced an even tone. (4) Beethoven composed for this style at first, but then his ideas changed. (5) People were astounded when he performed his music in the early 1800s. (6) There were crashing chords that frightened some of his audiences, and there were extreme changes in loudness and softness. (7) Beethoven sought sound effects that no one had ever thought possible. (8) The demands on the piano increased, and the instrument had to be changed. (9) It was not rare for pianos to break while they were being played forcefully. (10) Finally the modern piano evolved, and today's pianists use instruments that can produce a wide range of sounds and stand up to strong playing.

_____ 1. **A** simple
  B compound
  C complex
  D compound-complex

_____ 2. **A** simple
  B compound
  C complex
  D compound-complex

_____ 3. **A** simple
  B compound
  C complex
  D compound-complex

_____ 4. **A** simple
  B compound
  C complex
  D compound-complex

_____ 5. **A** simple
  B compound
  C complex
  D compound-complex

_____ 6. **A** simple
  B compound
  C complex
  D compound-complex

_____ 7. **A** simple
  B compound
  C complex
  D compound-complex

_____ 8. **A** simple
  B compound
  C complex
  D compound-complex

_____ 9. **A** simple
  B compound
  C complex
  D compound-complex

_____ 10. **A** simple
  B compound
  C complex
  D compound-complex

CHAPTER 18 Clauses Review

> **EXERCISE** Write the letter of the term that correctly identifies each sentence or the underlined part of the sentence.

---

(1) When I was ten years old, (2) I began learning how to play the ukulele. (3) Even though I struggled a bit at first, I had a lot of fun. The ukulele, (4) which comes from Hawaii, looks like a small guitar. (5) It has only four strings, and it produces a distinctive, happy sound when played. In middle school, people thought it was weird (6) that I played the ukulele. (7) Most kids were learning to play more traditional instruments like the violin or flute. (8) What other people think has never bothered me, however. Besides, there weren't many (9) who were laughing when I won the high school talent show. (10) After the show was over, I was talking to a classmate, and he even asked if I could give him ukulele lessons so that he could learn to play just like me.

_____ 1. **A** independent clause
    B adverbial clause
    C adjectival clause
    D noun clause

_____ 2. **A** independent clause
    B noun clause
    C restrictive clause
    D nonrestrictive clause

_____ 3. **A** simple sentence
    B compound sentence
    C complex sentence
    D compound-complex sentence

_____ 4. **A** restrictive clause
    B adverbial clause
    C adjectival clause
    D noun clause

_____ 5. **A** simple sentence
    B compound sentence
    C complex sentence
    D compound-complex sentence

_____ 6. **A** independent clause
    B adverbial clause
    C nonrestrictive clause
    D restrictive clause

_____ 7. **A** simple sentence
    B compound sentence
    C complex sentence
    D compound-complex sentence

_____ 8. **A** restrictive clause
    B adverbial clause
    C adjectival clause
    D noun clause

_____ 9. **A** adverbial clause
    B adjectival clause
    C nonrestrictive clause
    D noun clause

_____ 10. **A** simple sentence
    B compound sentence
    C complex sentence
    D compound-complex sentence

CHAPTER 19   Sentence Fragments

[19A] A **sentencefragment** is a group of words that does not express a complete thought.

EXERCISEWrite S if the group of words is a sentence or F if it is a fragment.

_____ 1. Plays piano very well.

_____ 2. My mother was playing the guitar.

_____ 3. The baby's toy is lost.

_____ 4. The baby's rubber toy.

_____ 5. The really interesting assembly yesterday.

_____ 6. We liked to rehearse before the assembly.

_____ 7. Walked all the way to the bus stop.

_____ 8. The children were finishing their tests.

_____ 9. The key was found in the kitchen.

_____ 10. The bottom drawer of the kitchen cabinet.

_____ 11. A young boy and girl.

_____ 12. He and I sang.

_____ 13. Ron liked to take a nap after lunch was over.

_____ 14. The fantastic lunch in the restaurant.

_____ 15. An hour and a half.

_____ 16. The team scored a run.

_____ 17. Scored a run after only six innings.

_____ 18. Please tie your shoe.

_____ 19. Heard a really good concert.

_____ 20. Cooked a terrific dinner this evening.

_____ 21. Red, purple, and blue are my favorite colors.

_____ 22. Wrote the word as clearly as possible.

CHAPTER 19 Sentence Fragments

EXERCISE Rewrite each fragment to make it a complete sentence. If the group of words is already a complete sentence, write *correct*.

1. The voting booths on the other side of the room.

   _____

2. A pencil, four sheets of paper, and a ruler.

   _____

3. Flew the kite on a very windy day.

   _____

4. I haven't spoken with him yet.

   _____

5. Took the bus to Haley Street.

   _____

6. Light bulbs, a hammer, and some tape.

   _____

7. We should leave in a little while.

   _____

8. Was supposed to fall on a Tuesday this year.

   _____

9. Look at the twinkling of the millions of stars.

   _____

10. Did whatever she wanted them to do.

    _____

11. My favorite breed of dog.

    _____

CHAPTER 19 Phrase Fragments

[19B.1] When phrases are written alone, they are called **phrasefragments** .

EXERCISEA Write *sentence* or *phrase fragment* to identify each group of words.

_____ 1. My bicycle can be repaired for fifteen dollars.

_____ 2. Speaking at the assembly for all ninth graders.

_____ 3. To think of something funny to say.

_____ 4. Mowing the lawn is my responsibility.

_____ 5. Put the groceries away.

_____ 6. Presenting the author of the play.

_____ 7. At ten o'clock on Friday, the meeting will be held.

_____ 8. There, on the corner of Evergreen Street.

EXERCISEB Rewrite each phrase fragment to make it a complete sentence. If the group of words is already a complete sentence, write *correct*.

---

9. Standing beneath the waterfall.

_____

10. To draw in art class.

_____

11. Needing a glass of water, I went inside.

_____

12. Before the American Revolution.

_____

13. Painted a pale yellow, the walls were pretty.

_____

··· CHAPTER 19 Clause Fragments

[19B.2] When a subordinate clause stands alone, it is known as a **clausefragment** .

> **EXERCISE**Decide whether each group of words is a sentence or a clause fragment.

_____ 1. After the painting was framed and hung on the wall.

    A sentence
    B clause fragment

_____ 2. That the witness told the police after the accident.

    A sentence
    B clause fragment

_____ 3. Before he left he spoke with her.

    A sentence
    B clause fragment

_____ 4. Dry the dishes while you're standing there.

    A sentence
    B clause fragment

_____ 5. After we know the results of the tests.

    A sentence
    B clause fragment

_____ 6. Who is the new captain of the football team?

    A sentence
    B clause fragment

_____ 7. While the weather is still cool.

    A sentence
    B clause fragment

_____ 8. Until we know, there's nothing to do.

    A sentence
    B clause fragment

_____ 9. She's the one who told me.

    A sentence
    B clause fragment

_____ 10. Even though we couldn't see well from the second balcony.

    A sentence
    B clause fragment

_____ 11. While I posed for the photographer.

    A sentence
    B clause fragment

_____ 12. After I raised my hand, I forgot my question.

    A sentence
    B clause fragment

_____ 13. To whom the package was addressed.

    A sentence
    B clause fragment

_____ 14. That I was telling you about.

    A sentence
    B clause fragment

_____ 15. Without the study sheet I had prepared.

    A sentence
    B clause fragment

_____ 16. Swabbing the deck, the sailor whistled.

    A sentence
    B clause fragment

_____ 17. Before the sun rose.

    A sentence
    B clause fragment

_____ 18. If we display an American flag on the Fourth of July.

    A sentence
    B clause fragment

CHAPTER 19 Clause Fragments

EXERCISE Rewrite each clause fragment to make it a complete sentence. If the group of words is already a complete sentence, write *correct*.

1. Whose sports equipment is lying out.

   _____

2. To whom do these shoes belong?

   _____

3. Plug in the CD player.

   _____

4. As I searched the Internet for information.

   _____

5. When we adopted our golden retriever, Missy.

   _____

6. Name the tune that is playing now.

   _____

7. Which was constructed in 1885.

   _____

8. Because he doubted me.

   _____

9. Since we needed paper, string, and tape.

   _____

10. Before dawn we rose.

   _____

11. High in the treehouse he had built.

   _____

CHAPTER 19 Run-on Sentences

[19C] Arun-onsentence is two or more sentences that are written together and are separated by a comma or no mark of punctuation at all.

EXERCISELabel each group of words S for sentence or R for run-on.

_____ 1. Armon has several pets they include two turtles and one hamster.

_____ 2. Those earrings are unusual, they are made of genuine jade.

_____ 3. The dance will be held at the Robinsons' barn, which is just off Old Raven Road.

_____ 4. I took skiing lessons the instructor has been skiing since she was three years old.

_____ 5. When you entered the room, did you notice the painting on the wall?

_____ 6. I have three favorite subjects they are French, history, and chorus.

_____ 7. Just as I was getting comfortable, my mother called me to do the dishes.

_____ 8. Have you ever ridden on a roller coaster, my cousin just loves them.

_____ 9. I have three brothers two of them are in college.

_____ 10. As long as you're going to the kitchen, please get me an apple.

_____ 11. The name *Sarah* means "princess," *Linda* means "beautiful."

_____ 12. The oldest subway system in the world is in London, it went into service in 1863.

_____ 13. I enjoyed reading the book; it was funny yet informative.

_____ 14. I heard the weather report, it is going to rain.

_____ 15. A fly has mosaic eyes, it can see in many different directions at the same time.

_____ 16. The coach shouted instructions, and the players responded immediately.

_____ 17. Flamingos are usually pink one variety is bright red.

_____ 18. My camera is old I'll be glad to get a new one.

CHAPTER 19 Run-on Sentences

EXERCISE Correct each run-on sentence by forming two sentences. If the sentence is not a run-on, write *correct*.

1. My father has a new job, it starts tomorrow.

   _____

2. Neil's shirt is blue because he likes that color.

   _____

3. Anna plays the violin, she is practicing now.

   _____

4. The car skidded luckily no one was near it.

   _____

5. If you go, Jo will go too, I will stay here.

   _____

6. Jack is changing the oil in his motorcycle, this must be done every 3,000 miles.

   _____

7. Because the recipe was difficult, Janine was reluctant to make the birthday cake.

   _____

8. Mrs. Utley postponed our field trip to the nature center since the weather report is predicting rain.

   _____

9. Unless we schedule several more hours of rehearsal, I'm afraid we won't be ready for Tuesday's performance.

   _____

10. Zoë should be ready for her nap at any moment, she's already stayed awake much longer than usual.

    _____

11. My little sister finally agreed to do the dishes for me because she wants to borrow my new outfit.

    _____

CHAPTER 19 Run-on Sentences

EXERCISE A Choose the best conjunction to connect the independent clauses below.

_____ 1. Wayne had climbed the tree, _____ he couldn't get down.
   A but
   B or

_____ 2. North Street is being repaired, _____ we went a different way.
   A for
   B so

_____ 3. Is Laura going to the party, _____ is she staying home?
   A yet
   B or

_____ 4. Jim is the hockey coach, _____ he is doing a good job.
   A and
   B for

_____ 5. The group sang well, _____ the music was not exciting.
   A but
   B so

_____ 6. Stephanie plans to visit me, _____ I won't be home.
   A and
   B but

_____ 7. Otto will bring dessert, _____ he might bring an appetizer.
   A or
   B but

_____ 8. That is a great movie, _____ this one is even better.
   A for
   B yet

EXERCISE B Write the best conjunction to connect the independent clauses below.

9. She told me I was crazy, _____ I'm going to have the last laugh.

10. We haven't written our speech yet, _____ we aren't finished with the research.

11. It is cold outside, _____ you still insist on running the ceiling fan!

12. Mary's favorite band is Low, _____ she does not have their new CD.

13. It seems that your kitten likes me, _____ she won't stop scratching my shoe!

14. I will try your carrot cake, _____ don't expect me to love it.

CHAPTER 19 Sentence Fragments and Run-ons Review

EXERCISERead the passage. Write the letter of the best way to write each underlined section. If the underlined section contains no error, write D.

Cricket is a sport played with a bat and **(1)** ball, somewhat like baseball. **(2)** Played on fields of three shapes: a circle, a square, or an oval. At the center of the field **(3)** is the pitch, two wickets are placed at either end. A wicket is **(4)** a target. That the batting team tries to defend. The other team's bowler, similar to a baseball **(5)** pitcher, who throws the ball at the batsman. Cricket teams each have eleven **(6)** players, the game is played mostly in **(7)** Britain. And in former British territories. A complete game of cricket can take up to **(8)** several days to finish. Matches at the amateur level, however, don't last as long. As is the case **(9)** with baseball. The goal of the game is to score more runs than the opposing team.

_____ 1. **A** ball. Somewhat like
 B ball, it is somewhat like
 C ball, yet it is somewhat like
 D No error

_____ 2. **A** Played on fields of three shapes.
 A circle, a square, or an oval.
 B It is played on fields of three shapes,
 the fields are a circle, a square, or an
 oval.
 C It is played on fields of three shapes: a
 circle, a square, or an oval.
 D No error

_____ 3. **A** is the pitch; two wickets are placed
 B is the pitch two wickets. Are placed
 C is the pitch two wickets are placed
 D No error

_____ 4. **A** a target that the batting team
 B a target, the batting team
 C a target, and the batting team
 D No error

_____ 5. **A** pitcher. Who throws
 B pitcher, is who throws
 C pitcher throwing
 D No error

_____ 6. **A** players, but the game
 B players the game
 C players. The game
 D No error

_____ 7. **A** Britain, in former British territories.
 B Britain and in former British
 territories.
 C Britain, and so in former British
 territories.
 D No error

_____ 8. **A** several days to finish matches
 B several days to finish, matches
 C several days. To finish matches
 D No error

_____ 9. **A** with baseball, and the goal of the
 game
 B with baseball, which is the goal of the
 game
 C with baseball, the goal of the game
 D No error

Name _____ Date _____

CHAPTER 20   The Principal Parts of a Verb

[20.A] The **principalparts** of a verb are the **present**, the **presentparticiple**, the **past** , and the **pastparticiple**.

EXERCISE A Identify the underlined verb as present, present participle, past, or past participle.

_____ 1. After the storm the sailboat <u>lay</u> on its side.

    A present
    B present participle
    C past
    D past participle

_____ 2. Every summer I <u>drive</u> my grandfather's tractor.

    A present
    B present participle
    C past
    D past participle

_____ 3. Deirdre <u>won</u> first place in the marathon.

    A present
    B present participle
    C past
    D past participle

_____ 4. Mr. Foster <u>is growing</u> his own vegetables.

    A present
    B present participle
    C past
    D past participle

_____ 5. The birds <u>have eaten</u> all the suet we put out.

    A present
    B present participle
    C past
    D past participle

_____ 6. After you <u>have set</u> the table, call everyone to dinner.

    A present
    B present participle
    C past
    D past participle

EXERCISEB Underline the verb in each sentence. Then label it as present, present participle, past, or past participle.

_____ 7. The police officer told us about crime prevention.

_____ 8. I have never found my watch.

_____ 9. The cake rose above the sides of the pan.

_____ 10. Amanda has left her cashier's job at the mall.

_____ 11. Lucia got the majority of the votes.

_____ 12. He is drawing me a map of the fairgrounds.

_____ 13. The judges of the contest haven't chosen a winner yet.

_____ 14. I run at the track every day after school.

CHAPTER 20 Irregular Verbs

[20A.2] An **irregularverb** does not form its past and past participle by adding *-ed* or *-d* to the present form.

EXERCISE Choose the correct verb form to complete each sentence.

_____ 1. All the balloons had _____ by the time the party ended.

    A bursted
    B burst

_____ 2. Ms. Jarvis _____ both chemistry and biology last year.

    A teached
    B taught

_____ 3. What topic have you _____ for your report?

    A chosen
    B choosed

_____ 4. The outfielder _____ the ball to first base for the third out.

    A throwed
    B threw

_____ 5. By the time the concert _____, the auditorium was full.

    A began
    B begun

_____ 6. The robin had _____ three worms by sunrise.

    A eaten
    B ate

_____ 7. Has Mr. Lanza's class _____ the test yet?

    A taken
    B took

_____ 8. The cheerleaders _____ red-and-white striped outfits.

    A weared
    B wore

_____ 9. The bell _____ before Martin had finished writing.

    A rang
    B rung

_____ 10. We have _____ thirty miles.

    A drove
    B driven

_____ 11. After their long trip, they finally _____ home.

    A have come
    B have came

_____ 12. Who _____ London Bridge from England?

    A buy
    B bought

_____ 13. Those skaters have _____ gold medals.

    A win
    B won

_____ 14. Has anyone _____ any tickets to the book fair?

    A bought
    B buying

_____ 15. The weeds have _____ very tall.

    A grew
    B grown

_____ 16. The melon rind _____ soft to the touch.

    A felt
    B feeled

_____ 17. The guide dog _____ with its owner on the bus.

    A sit
    B sat

_____ 18. Divers have _____ treasure ships off the Florida coast.

    A found
    B founded

CHAPTER 20   Irregular Verbs

EXERCISECross out the underlined verb form in each sentence, and write the correct form above it.

1. The team members just <u>choose</u> a mascot.

2. Play rehearsals have not <u>began</u> yet.

3. My sister has <u>drove</u> to Boston many times.

4. Mr. Beck has <u>grew</u> corn for years.

5. The quarterback <u>thrown</u> a 50-yard pass.

6. Luis may have just <u>broke</u> a window.

7. No one has <u>saw</u> our new neighbors.

8. My hat has never <u>fell</u> into the lake before.

9. The pond has finally <u>froze</u> over.

10. Polly <u>drunk</u> all the orange juice.

11. Has the boat <u>sank</u> to the bottom?

12. I have just <u>wrote</u> for a free sample.

CHAPTER 20   Problem Verbs

[20B.1] *Lie* means "to rest or recline." *Lie* is never followed by a direct object. *Lay* means "to put or set (something) down." *Lay* is usually followed by a direct object.

[20B.2] *Rise* means "to move upward" or "to get up." *Rise* is never followed by a direct object. *Raise* means "to lift (something) up," "to increase," or "to grow something." *Raise* is usually followed by a direct object.

[20B.3] *Sit* means "to rest in an upright position." *Sit* is never followed by a direct object. *Set* usually means "to put or place (something)." *Set* is usually followed by a direct object.

EXERCISE Circle the verb that correctly completes each sentence.

---

1. Don't (lay, lie) in the sun for too long.

2. The Loch Ness monster (rose, raised) from the lake.

3. Yesterday Marguerite (sat, set) pots of herbs on the windowsill.

4. Try to be quiet while the children are (lying, laying) down for a nap.

5. Each morning Vinod (rises, raises) the flag in front of the school.

6. Despite the sign, the man (set, sat) in the wet paint on the bench.

7. The delivery person has (lain, laid) the packages on the front table.

8. Wow! Your grades have (raised, risen) quite a bit.

9. An employee is (setting, sitting) all the sale items together on a table.

10. The workers are (lying, laying) bricks for a retaining wall.

11. The price of gasoline had (rose, risen) again.

12. I had (sat, set) at the bus stop for ten minutes before a bus came.

13. These rugs have (lain, laid) on our floors for twenty years.

14. A system of chains and pulleys (raises, rises) the bridge.

15. My cousin will be (setting, sitting) next to me at the awards banquet.

16. Will you (lay, lie) out the patterns and bolts of fabric?

17. Fay (rose, raised) cattle on her ranch.

18. Why is my good dress (lying, laying) on the floor, Sis?

CHAPTER 20 Problem Verbs

> **EXERCISE** Cross out the underlined verb in each sentence and write the correct form above it.

1. Do you mind if I <u>set</u> here?

2. The blood donor felt faint and <u>laid</u> back to rest.

3. He <u>raised</u> on time and got to work promptly.

4. After the boat ride, I was happy to <u>sit</u> foot on land again.

5. Tell Robbie he should <u>lay</u> on the sofa and keep the injured foot up.

6. The lake level began <u>raising</u> during the heavy rains.

7. Have you <u>sat</u> the trash bags by the curb yet?

8. By noon, Nina had <u>lain</u> all of the tile for the kitchen floor.

9. The Girl Scouts are <u>rising</u> money by selling cookies.

10. The hen is <u>setting</u> on her eggs.

11. The volleyball net is <u>laying</u> in a heap over there.

12. The price of the soft drinks in the machine has <u>rose</u>.

13. <u>Lie</u> your coats on the bed.

CHAPTER 20 Identifying Tenses

[20C] The time expressed by a verb is called the **tense** of a verb.

[20C.1] The six tenses of a verb are the **present**, **past**, **future**, **presentperfect** , **pastperfect** , and **futureperfect**.

EXERCISE Choose the correct tense of the underlined verb.

_____ 1. He and I <u>walk</u> to school.

    A past
    B present

_____ 2. They <u>marched</u> across the lawn.

    A past
    B past perfect

_____ 3. Becky <u>is trying</u> hard.

    A present participle
    B future

_____ 4. I <u>have looked</u> there already.

    A present
    B past participle

_____ 5. Max finally <u>called</u> Mrs. Silva.

    A past
    B past perfect

_____ 6. They <u>are cooking</u> dinner right now.

    A present participle
    B past participle

_____ 7. They <u>row</u> on the lake almost every weekend.

    A past participle
    B present

_____ 8. Jan <u>has read</u> it.

    A past participle
    B past

_____ 9. Our team <u>won</u> last night.

    A past
    B present

_____ 10. Howard <u>has used</u> it for math.

    A present
    B past participle

_____ 11. The police officer <u>checked</u> the alley behind the store.

    A past
    B past perfect

_____ 12. My mother and father <u>weigh</u> themselves once a week.

    A present
    B future

_____ 13. No one <u>has wrapped</u> Angel's gift yet.

    A past perfect
    B present perfect

_____ 14. After Gil <u>had cooked</u> the soup, he remembered the carrots.

    A past
    B past perfect

_____ 15. The Chens <u>will</u> probably <u>have</u> the cast party at their house.

    A future perfect
    B future

_____ 16. By Friday they <u>will have reached</u> Dallas.

    A future perfect
    B past perfect

_____ 17. The actress <u>has</u> always <u>taken</u> a short nap before each show.

    A present perfect
    B past

_____ 18. Until she visited her aunt, Fay <u>had</u> never <u>seen</u> the ocean.

    A past perfect
    B present perfect

CHAPTER 20 Identifying Tenses

EXERCISE Label the tense of each underlined verb.

_____ 1. <u>Have</u> you ever <u>seen</u> the eagle?

_____ 2. <u>Will</u> you <u>sneeze</u> during class today?

_____ 3. What color <u>are</u> your socks?

_____ 4. By 5:30 this evening, how long <u>will</u> you <u>have been</u> awake?

_____ 5. <u>Was</u> there anything green in your closet this morning?

_____ 6. The Winter Olympics <u>provides</u> skaters with an ideal opportunity.

_____ 7. Every pair <u>hopes</u> for a gold medal for their performance.

_____ 8. Years of preparation and rehearsal <u>lie</u> behind each act.

_____ 9. Jayne Torvill and Christopher Dean <u>entered</u> the Winter Olympics in Yugoslavia.

_____ 10. They <u>represented</u> Great Britain in the figure skating events.

_____ 11. Before the judges and audience, they <u>performed</u> a beautiful dance.

_____ 12. For the first time, a skating routine <u>earned</u> a perfect score.

_____ 13. The English people <u>remember</u> Torvill and Dean with great pride.

_____ 14. Future Olympics <u>will provide</u> other skaters with gold medals.

_____ 15. Before the phonograph most people <u>had heard</u> only live music.

_____ 16. By 1930, most Americans <u>had listened</u> to phonograph records.

_____ 17. During World War II, jukeboxes <u>had become</u> popular.

_____ 18. Today everyone <u>has listened</u> to music in banks, stores, and even dentists' offices.

_____ 19. Today people <u>test</u> the effect of music on plants.

CHAPTER 20 Progressive Verb Forms

[20C.3] Each of the six verb tenses has a **progressive** form. The progressive form is used to express continuing or ongoing action. To form the progressive, add a form of the *be* verb to the present participle.

EXERCISEA For each word, choose the verb form given in parentheses.

_____ 1. sing (present progressive)
   A was singing
   B will have been singing
   C is singing
   D had been singing

_____ 2. swim (future progressive)
   A will be swimming
   B had been swimming
   C has been swimming
   D is swimming

_____ 3. sink (past perfect progressive)
   A has been sinking
   B had been sinking
   C will have been sinking
   D was sinking

_____ 4. dig (future perfect progressive)
   A is digging
   B will be digging
   C had been digging
   D will have been digging

_____ 5. shine (past progressive)
   A was shining
   B had been shining
   C has been shining
   D will have been shining

_____ 6. drink (present perfect progressive)
   A is drinking
   B had been drinking
   C has been drinking
   D will have been drinking

_____ 7. write (present progressive)
   A was writing
   B will have been writing
   C has been writing
   D is writing

_____ 8. race (future perfect progressive)
   A will be racing
   B was racing
   C will have been racing
   D had been racing

EXERCISEB Choose the verb that is in the specified verb form.

_____ 9. present progressive
   A has been clapping
   B will be walking
   C are laughing
   D was whispering

_____ 10. past perfect progressive
   A were kissing
   B had been sledding
   C have been promising
   D shall have been skipping

continued

Chapter 20: **Progressive Verb Forms** *continued*

_____ 11. past progressive
  A had been shooting
  B was floating
  C is jogging
  D has been calling

_____ 12. future perfect progressive
  A will have been sleeting
  B was bicycling
  C has been whistling
  D will be typing

_____ 13. future progressive
  A is mowing
  B has been fishing
  C will have been driving
  D will be trading

_____ 14. present perfect progressive
  A will have been barking
  B has been mopping
  C were jumping
  D had been giggling

CHAPTER 20 Progressive Verb Forms

EXERCISE Write each underlined verb in the form that is indicated in parentheses.

_____ 1. Until now, I perform (*past perfect progressive*) well.

_____ 2. We have (*present progressive*) a garage sale.

_____ 3. Captain Galdamez fly (*future progressive*) the jet.

_____ 4. Sonny do (*present perfect progressive*) homework for two hours.

_____ 5. She ski (*past progressive*) when she broke her leg.

_____ 6. By five o'clock, we practice (*future perfect progressive*) for three hours.

_____ 7. I sweep (*past progressive*) the floor when I found the bracelet.

_____ 8. The principal encourage (*present perfect progressive*) us.

_____ 9. Nadia style (*present progressive*) her hair.

_____ 10. Leon study (*past perfect progressive*) the stars through a telescope.

_____ 11. We dance (*future progressive*) till the band goes home.

_____ 12. By February, Keisha serve (*future perfect progressive*) as class president for six months.

CHAPTER 20 Shifts in Tense

[20C.4] Avoid unnecessary shifts in tense within a sentence or with related sentences.

EXERCISEA Write *YES* if the sentence has an unnecessary and incorrect shift in verb tense and *NO* if it does not.

_____ 1. That large motorboat always slows down before it stopped at the dock.

_____ 2. Chris walked bravely to the front of the room and faces his classmates.

_____ 3. The kitten stalked into the room and pounced on the rubber mouse.

_____ 4. After I had begun to mow the lawn, the rain starts.

_____ 5. The sightseeing boat leaves at noon and returned at three o'clock.

_____ 6. The halfback lost his balance but hung onto the ball.

_____ 7. Huge jets always pass directly over our house and headed west.

_____ 8. After I had seen the movie, I told everyone about it.

_____ 9. We park the car at the curb and jump out.

EXERCISEB Rewrite each sentence to correct an unnecessary and incorrect shift in verb tense.

10. When Cider ran away, Ken searches for him everywhere.

_____

11. I had played the video game before I order it.

_____

12. I walked into the restaurant and see a beautiful girl.

_____

13. Last week we were camping and catch fish for our dinner.

_____

14. Each evening the wind blows through the trees and rattled my window.

_____

15. My grandmother gives me a necklace, and I lost it.

_____

CHAPTER 20   Shifts in Tense

EXERCISE Choose the word group that completes the sentence without an incorrect shift in tense.

_____ 1. I was reading a story
   A and notice a spider on my arm.
   B and noticed a spider on my arm.

_____ 2. The girls call their moms
   A and then are going to the movie.
   B and then go to the movie.

_____ 3. Sometimes I yell at a friend
   A and then felt bad.
   B and then feel bad.

_____ 4. I built a sandcastle,
   A but the waves demolished it.
   B but the waves demolish it.

_____ 5. Ms. Garber said we could take the test immediately,
   A or we were reviewing first.
   B or we could review first.

_____ 6. The dog was yelping,
   A so I knew something was wrong.
   B so I knew something is wrong.

_____ 7. The war ended,
   A and peace reigned.
   B and peace was reigning.

_____ 8. I looked across the cafeteria,
   A but I see no one to sit with.
   B but I saw no one to sit with.

_____ 9. Show me the math problem,
   A and I will help you with it.
   B and I help you with it.

_____ 10. When the vehicle was new,
   A it had shiny white paint.
   B it was having shiny white paint.

_____ 11. The drummer has suggested a change in the song,
   A and the other band members agree.
   B and the other band members agreed.

_____ 12. I was laughing so hard
   A that tears will be running out of my eyes.
   B that tears were running out of my eyes.

_____ 13. When darkness fell,
   A the lights on the pier came on.
   B the lights on the pier come on.

_____ 14. We can either ride the Ferris wheel
   A or get some cotton candy.
   B or getting some cotton candy.

_____ 15. The hermit crab searched for a bigger shell,
   A yet no empty one has been in sight.
   B yet no empty one was in sight.

Name   Date

CHAPTER 20   Active and Passive Voice

[20D.1] The **activevoice** indicates that the subject is performing the action.

[20D.2] The **passivevoice** indicates that the action of the verb is being performed upon the subject.

EXERCISEA   Write *A* if the sentence is in the active voice or *P* if it is in the passive voice.

_____ 1. Ancient ruins have been discovered in our backyard.

_____ 2. The White House has 132 rooms.

_____ 3. Some businesses are guarded at night by watchdogs.

_____ 4. Jupiter's moons can be seen with good binoculars.

_____ 5. Dry the dishes with that towel.

_____ 6. The Gulf Stream warms the west coast of Europe.

_____ 7. The dog left a trail of muddy footprints.

_____ 8. Jade can be shattered by a sharp blow.

_____ 9. Tonight I must write a report for science class.

_____ 10. Computers are used to predict the monthly rainfall over the next five years.

EXERCISEB   Rewrite each sentence to be in the active voice.

---

11. James is always called Jim by his family.

_____

12. The lead part was played by Jayne.

_____

13. The rain was followed by a terrible thunderstorm.

_____

14. Two dimes were found by Bart under the cushions of the sofa.

_____

15. The bark on our trees is chewed by many deer.

_____

Copyright © Perfection Learning® All rights reserved.
Grade 9 • Chapter 20: Using Verbs   **121**

Name _____   Date _____

CHAPTER 20 **Using Verbs Review**

EXERCISE Read the passage and write the letter of the word or group of words that belong in each underlined space.

From the beginning, airplanes **(1)** _____ runways to take off and land. But in wartime, airfields **(2)** _____ easy targets, so armies **(3)** _____ looking for ways to fly planes without them. One approach was called "zero length launch." Instead of speeding down a runway, planes **(4)** _____ into the air by rockets. However, the launch platforms **(5)** _____ too costly and cumbersome, and runways were still needed by the planes to land.

Later, the Harrier Jump Jet was introduced by a British aircraft manufacturer. The Harrier **(6)** _____ thrust vectoring, in which the engines' thrust can be directed downward. The Harrier **(7)** _____ straight up from the ground, hover, and land without a runway.

Of course, if the military had been interested in just those capabilities, it could simply have used a helicopter. Helicopters **(8)** _____ for a century and use rotors rather than jet engines to create thrust. These versatile vehicles **(9)** _____ for everything from combat to tourism. But the helicopter has one major disadvantage compared to the Harrier: its speed. The fastest helicopter **(10)** _____ at about 200 miles per hour, while the Harrier reaches more than 700.

_____ 1. **A** require
 B have required
 C will require
 D will have required

_____ 2. **A** are
 B were being
 C being
 D will be

_____ 3. **A** begun
 B did begin
 C began
 D will have begun

_____ 4. **A** have been launched
 B have launched
 C were launched
 D launching

_____ 5. **A** proven
 B are proven
 C prove
 D proved

_____ 6. **A** utilizes
 B has been utilizing
 C utilize
 D will utilize

continued

Chapter 20: Using Verbs Review *continued*

_____ 7. **A** can raise
     B can rise
     C was raising
     D was rising

_____ 8. **A** exist
     B have existed
     C will have existed
     D were existing

_____ 9. **A** been used
     B used
     C will be used
     D have been used

_____ 10. **A** is traveling
     B has been traveling
     C travels
     D traveling

Name   Date

Determining the Case of Pronouns

[21A] Case is the form of a noun or a pronoun that indicates its use in a sentence.

[21A.1] The **nominativecase** is used for subjects and predicate nominatives.

[21A.3] Objectpronouns are used as direct objects, indirect objects, and objects of prepositions.

[21A.5] The **possessivecase** is used to show ownership or possession.

EXERCISEA Choose the correct case of each underlined pronoun.

_____ 1. Did Carlos find <u>his</u> sneakers?
  A nominative
  B objective
  C possessive

_____ 2. <u>They</u> were in the locker room.
  A nominative
  B objective
  C possessive

_____ 3. <u>We</u> rang for the elevator.
  A nominative
  B objective
  C possessive

_____ 4. <u>She</u> lives on the fifth floor.
  A nominative
  B objective
  C possessive

_____ 5. <u>Her</u> apartment number is 5G.
  A nominative
  B objective
  C possessive

_____ 6. Mrs. Collins called <u>us</u>.
  A nominative
  B objective
  C possessive

_____ 7. Willie waved to <u>me</u>.
  A nominative
  B objective
  C possessive

_____ 8. Tracy and <u>I</u> are working together.
  A nominative
  B objective
  C possessive

EXERCISEB Underline the pronoun in each sentence. Then label the case of the pronoun on the line provided.

_____ 9. A sparrow made its nest there.

_____ 10. Adam showed them the pictures.

_____ 11. Is the record for him?

_____ 12. The audience enjoyed her singing.

_____ 13. Please tell them the news.

_____ 14. The winners were she and Ralph.

_____ 15. The dog barked at her and Ray.

_____ 16. Is the basketball yours?

Name _____   Date _____

CHAPTER 21 Determining the Case of Pronouns

EXERCISE A From each pair, choose the sentence that correctly uses a personal pronoun.

_____ 1. **A** He really plays the guitar well.
   B Him really plays the guitar well.

_____ 2. **A** Sue and he both play well.
   B Sue and him both play well.

_____ 3. **A** Everyone enjoys them playing.
   B Everyone enjoys their playing.

_____ 4. **A** Both brought they're guitars.
   B Both brought their guitars.

_____ 5. **A** Ask they to play something.
   B Ask them to play something.

_____ 6. **A** Ask Mike and she to sing.
   B Ask Mike and her to sing.

_____ 7. **A** The electric guitar is hers.
   B The electric guitar is her's.

_____ 8. **A** Who will sing with them?
   B Who will sing with they?

_____ 9. **A** Who will sing with Cara and him?
   B Who will sing with Cara and he?

_____ 10. **A** The best singer is Bill or her.
   B The best singer is Bill or she.

EXERCISE B Indicate the case of the pronoun in each sentence you marked as correct for (1–10) above.

_____ 1. **A** nominative
   B objective
   C possessive

_____ 2. **A** nominative
   B objective
   C possessive

_____ 3. **A** nominative
   B objective
   C possessive

_____ 4. **A** nominative
   B objective
   C possessive

_____ 5. **A** nominative
   B objective
   C possessive

_____ 6. **A** nominative
   B objective
   C possessive

_____ 7. **A** nominative
   B objective
   C possessive

_____ 8. **A** nominative
   B objective
   C possessive

_____ 9. **A** nominative
   B objective
   C possessive

_____ 10. **A** nominative
   B objective
   C possessive

Name _____   Date _____

CHAPTER 21 **Using Pronouns Correctly**

> **EXERCISE** Circle the correct pronoun or pronouns for each sentence.

1. My family and (me / I) visited our cousins in Denver last week.

2. When playing with Corey or me, the cat never used (its / it's) claws.

3. Mrs. Wu and he approved of (them / they) working in the bank.

4. Is that leather belt (yours / your's), mine, or hers?

5. They told Ethel and (I / me) all about their new apartment.

6. On Friday Ted and (me / I) took Bea and (her / she) to the Pizza Palace.

7. Our uncle invited (us / we) nephews to (his / him) farm for our vacation.

8. At noon (us / we) marchers will assemble in the yard next to (your / you) house.

9. (Him / His) being late was not (him / his) fault but ours.

10. The three photographers were Ken, Becky, and (me / I).

11. Mary called to tell (she / her) about the storm.

12. After the picnic (us / we) hiked in the woods.

126   Grade 9 • Chapter 21: Using Pronouns   Copyright © Perfection Learning® All rights reserved.

CHAPTER 21 Substituting Pronouns for Nouns

EXERCISE Replace the underlined nouns with the most appropriate pronouns.

1. Mr. Kelly lent a bicycle built for two to Kevin and <u>Lillian</u>.

   _____

2. Tom and Sal took <u>Tom and Sal's</u> triplets for a walk in the park.

   _____

3. <u>Bill</u> and his mother finally found a pair of shoes that fit him.

   _____

4. We applauded <u>the acrobats'</u> somersaulting from one side of the stage to the other.

   _____

5. Benjamin told Ward and <u>Alice</u> the most incredible story.

   _____

6. After the play the director and <u>Lana</u> congratulated each other.

   _____

7. The stars of the evening were undoubtedly <u>Lana</u> and Bruce.

   _____

8. To Mrs. Cohen and <u>Leroy</u> go our thanks for a splendid evening.

   _____

9. <u>Maxine's</u> winning the race was a surprise to everyone but me.

   _____

10. With Harris and <u>Richard</u> on the team, we cannot lose.

    _____

11. <u>Maurice's</u> surprise was a new puppy from Petra.

    _____

12. We sat quietly as <u>the lone deer</u> walked past us in the woods.

    _____

CHAPTER 21 Using the Correct Form of *Who*

[21B.2] Forms of *who* are often used in questions. Use who when the pronoun is used as a subject. Use *whom* when the pronoun is used as a direct object or object of the preposition.

EXERCISE A Identify the correct form of *who* for each sentence.

_____ 1. _____ was driving the white convertible between 8:00 and 8:30 P.M.?

    A Who
    B Whom
    C Whose

_____ 2. Does Mr. VanDeLouis know to _____ the convertible actually belongs?

    A who
    B whom
    C whose

_____ 3. _____ fingerprints were on the dog's rhinestone collar?

    A Who
    B Whom
    C Whose

_____ 4. _____ did Mrs. VanDeLouis inform that she was going out?

    A Who
    B Whom
    C Whose

_____ 5. Will Mrs. VanDeLouis tell _____ borrowed her emerald tiara?

    A who
    B whom
    C whose

_____ 6. Will laboratory tests reveal _____ right shoe was left in the convertible?

    A who
    B whom
    C whose

_____ 7. Is Mr. VanDeLouis concealing _____ he saw in the hallway?

    A who
    B whom
    C whose

_____ 8. At _____ did the dog bark at 7:52 P.M.?

    A who
    B whom
    C whose

EXERCISE B Circle the correct form of *who*. Then indicate the use of each form (nominative, objective, or possessive.)

9. (Who / Whom) turned off the light?

_____

10. (Who / Whom) did they see on the bus?

_____

11. (Who / Whom) was on the bus?

_____

continued

Chapter 21: Using the Correct Form of *Who* continued

12. To (who / whom) are you waving?

     _____

13. (Who's / Whose) camera is this?

     _____

14. (Who's / Whose) red hat is on the seat?

     _____

15. (Who / Whom) did you ask to the party?

     _____

CHAPTER 21 — Determining the Case of *Who* in Questions

EXERCISE Select the answer that tells how the underlined word in each sentence is used.

_____ 1. Who is the new student?

    A subject
    B direct object
    C object of a preposition
    D possessive

_____ 2. Whom did you meet?

    A subject
    B direct object
    C object of a preposition
    D possessive

_____ 3. With whom do you wish to speak?

    A subject
    B direct object
    C object of a preposition
    D possessive

_____ 4. Whose stereo is that?

    A subject
    B direct object
    C object of a preposition
    D possessive

_____ 5. To whom did you send that postcard?

    A subject
    B direct object
    C object of a preposition
    D possessive

_____ 6. Whom did you tell about Basil's party?

    A subject
    B direct object
    C object of a preposition
    D possessive

_____ 7. Whose suitcase is sitting on the porch?

    A subject
    B direct object
    C object of a preposition
    D possessive

_____ 8. With whom did you sit at the Breakers concert?

    A subject
    B direct object
    C object of a preposition
    D possessive

_____ 9. Who is the man with the straw hat and sunglasses?

    A subject
    B direct object
    C object of a preposition
    D possessive

_____ 10. Whom did Lillian meet at the lecture?

    A subject
    B direct object
    C object of a preposition
    D possessive

Name _____   Date _____

CHAPTER 21 Using Forms of *Who* in Clauses

[21B.3] The form of *who* you use depends on how the pronoun is used within the clause. Use *who* when the pronoun is used as the subject of the clause. Use *whom* when the pronoun is used as a direct object or object of the preposition in the clause.

EXERCISEA Choose the form of *who* that will correctly complete each sentence.

_____ 1. Melba didn't know _____ sent the flowers.
    A who
    B whom

_____ 2. The club accepts _____ wants to join.
    A whoever
    B whomever

_____ 3. Sam couldn't tell to _____ she was referring.
    A who
    B whom

_____ 4. _____ answers the phone should take messages.
    A Whoever
    B Whomever

_____ 5. Did Gene know _____ the judge was?
    A who
    B whom

_____ 6. The person _____ they select will get a screen test.
    A who
    B whom

EXERCISEB Circle the form of *who* that will correctly complete each sentence.

7. (Whoever / Whomever) is the sixth caller wins one hundred dollars.

8. No one questioned (who / whom) made that decision.

9. Everyone admires the person (who / whom) you are.

10. This is Willie, to (who / whom) all the credit must be given.

11. The parade was led by two drum majors (who / whom) were dressed in white and gold.

12. Glenn Carlson, (who / whom) is the team's best runner, sprained his ankle.

13. Two men, one of (who / whom) dived into the icy water, are responsible for saving the boy's life.

14. Take (whoever / whomever) you need to get the job done.

15. I spoke with the people from (who / whom) I had received the invitation.

Pronouns in Comparisons

[21B.4] In an **ellipticalclause** , use the form of the pronoun you would use if the clause were completed.

EXERCISECircle the pronoun that correctly completes the sentence.

---

1. Greg spends more time with them than with (I / me).

2. Do you think I'm as tall as (he / him)?

3. Our teacher didn't review the test with us as much as with (they / them).

4. Is Toby as old as (she / her)?

5. I studied longer than (they / them).

6. The tennis tournament seemed more exciting to them than to (we / us).

7. Helmut lifts as many weights as (he / him).

8. I think Marvin is a better singer than (she / her).

9. Our cat means more to Shelby than to (I / me).

10. Hayes likes hot weather as much as (they / them).

11. Everyone should be as cheerful as (he / him).

12. Did you collect as many old newspapers as (they / them)?

13. I think Robin can run faster than (I / me).

14. The people from the television station talked longer to us than to (they / them).

15. At the school crafts fair last week, no one worked harder than (we / us).

16. This chef is more experienced than (she / her).

17. I usually spend less time doing homework than (he / him).

18. I admitted that he was a better golfer than (I / me).

19. We were more interested in the exhibit than (they / them).

CHAPTER 21 • Pronouns in Comparisons

EXERCISE Choose the sentence that correctly completes the elliptical comparison.

_____ 1. I like salty foods more than _____.

    A I like salty foods more than she likes them.

    B I like salty foods more than her likes them.

_____ 2. Ned does more chores than _____.

    A Ned does more chores than they do.

    B Ned does more chores than them do.

_____ 3. Chrissie likes Ty as a science partner more than _____.

    A Chrissie likes Ty as a science partner more than them do.

    B Chrissie likes Ty as a science partner more than she likes them.

_____ 4. I called Charlie sooner than _____.

    A I called Charlie sooner than her did.

    B I called Charlie sooner than I called her.

_____ 5. My older sister has a later curfew than _____.

    A My older sister has a later curfew than me do.

    B My older sister has a later curfew than I do.

_____ 6. Carlos reads much faster than _____.

    A Carlos reads much faster than her does.

    B Carlos reads much faster than she does.

_____ 7. Mom checked on the baby earlier than _____.

    A Mom checked on the baby earlier than they did.

    B Mom checked on the baby earlier than them did.

_____ 8. Do you like coconut cake as much as _____?

    A Do you like coconut cake as much as I do?

    B Do you like coconut cake as much as me do?

_____ 9. I will try to be as honest as _____.

    A I will try to be as honest as them were.

    B I will try to be as honest as they were.

_____ 10. Serena is happier than _____.

    A Serena is happier than he is.

    B Serena is happier than him is.

_____ 11. I sent invitations to them before _____.

    A I sent invitations to them before I sent one to she.

    B I sent invitations to them before I sent one to her.

_____ 12. At the track meet, I jumped as far as _____.

    A At the track meet, I jumped as far as him did.

    B At the track meet, I jumped as far as he did.

_____ 13. Chad saw Mallory sooner than _____.

    A Chad saw Mallory sooner than he saw they.

    B Chad saw Mallory sooner than he saw them.

_____ 14. Kevin enjoyed the dinner more than _____.

    A Kevin enjoyed the dinner more than her enjoyed the dinner.

    B Kevin enjoyed the dinner more than she did.

CHAPTER 21   Pronouns and Their Antecedents

[21C] A pronoun must agree in **number** and **gender** with its antecedent.

[21C.1] Number is the term used to indicate whether a noun or pronoun is singular or plural. Singular indicates one, and plural indicates more than one. **Gender** is the term used to indicate whether a noun or a pronoun is masculine, feminine, or neuter.

EXERCISEA   Choose the pronoun that agrees with its antecedent(s) in each sentence.

_____ 1. A slow caterpillar and a speedy ant made _____ separate ways around and around the tree trunk.
  - **A** his
  - **B** their
  - **C** my
  - **D** they

_____ 2. Neither the woman with the suitcase nor the girl with the guitar has bought _____ bus ticket yet.
  - **A** her
  - **B** their
  - **C** she
  - **D** its

_____ 3. Everybody on the boys' swim team has placed _____ order for a team jacket.
  - **A** his
  - **B** their
  - **C** he
  - **D** its

_____ 4. None of the magazines in the doctor's waiting room still have all _____ pages.
  - **A** his
  - **B** their
  - **C** its
  - **D** it's

_____ 5. Most of the salad in the refrigerator has lost _____ original color.
  - **A** his
  - **B** their
  - **C** it's
  - **D** its

CHAPTER 21   Pronouns and Their Antecedents

EXERCISE B Decide whether the underlined pronoun agrees with its antecedent.

_____ 6. Either Bart or Joe left <u>their</u> lunch in the library.
- **A** yes
- **B** no

_____ 7. All camera-club members should choose five of <u>their</u> best pictures for the exhibit.
- **A** yes
- **B** no

_____ 8. Otis and Roy will give <u>their</u> speeches tomorrow.
- **A** yes
- **B** no

_____ 9. Neither Ruth nor Virginia remembered <u>their</u> key.
- **A** yes
- **B** no

_____ 10. Nathan took five suitcases with <u>him</u> to Florida.
- **A** yes
- **B** no

_____ 11. All players were responsible for <u>his</u> own uniforms.
- **A** yes
- **B** no

_____ 12. After the Cases bought the house, <u>they</u> painted it.
- **A** yes
- **B** no

_____ 13. Dad carried the groceries and put <u>it</u> in the car.
- **A** yes
- **B** no

_____ 14. A robin built <u>their</u> nest near the back porch.
- **A** yes
- **B** no

_____ 15. Either Kate or Sue will play <u>her</u> own sonata.
- **A** yes
- **B** no

Name _____   Date _____

CHAPTER 21 Pronouns and Their Antecedents

EXERCISE Correct the underlined pronoun to agree with its antecedent.

_____ 1. Each of the girls won <u>their</u> school letter.

_____ 2. All of the trees in our yard have lost <u>its</u> leaves.

_____ 3. No one on the girls' team likes <u>their</u> uniform.

_____ 4. Many of the citizens cast <u>his or her</u> votes early.

_____ 5. Some of the cheese has lost <u>their</u> flavor.

_____ 6. Neither of the girls received <u>their</u> driver's license.

_____ 7. Several of the employees bring <u>his or her</u> lunches.

_____ 8. Someone in the boys' choir had forgotten <u>their</u> part.

_____ 9. One of the bridesmaids lost <u>their</u> bouquet.

_____ 10. Both of the Schlaffman twins jog on the path near <u>his</u> home.

_____ 11. Someone in the audience began clapping <u>their</u> hands.

_____ 12. Few of the students completed <u>his or her</u> assignment on time.

_____ 13. One of the girls will give <u>their</u> report next.

_____ 14. When Alison and Jeffrey arrived, <u>she</u> gave the hostess a gift.

_____ 15. Some of the bread has mold on <u>their</u> surface.

Name _____ Date _____

CHAPTER 21 **Using Pronouns Review**

EXERCISE In the paragraph below, some of the underlined pronouns are incorrect. Write the correct form of the pronoun on the lines below. If the pronoun is correct, write C on the line.

When Miss Lin announced that the fall play at school would be *Romeo and Juliet,* we were shocked. None of **(1)** we students expected **(2)** her to pick a play by Shakespeare. Jackie, Kim, and **(3)** me decided to audition. Kim and I think Jackie is a better actress than **(4)** us. We encouraged **(5)** she to try out for the part of Juliet. Some of the boys said **(6)** he might audition for the part of Romeo. At the audition, each student had to read **(7)** their favorite scene from the play. When Jackie finished reading, the audience clapped **(8)** its hands. Both Jackie and another girl were called back to read **(9)** her scenes again. Later, we waited in the hall outside the theater. **(10)** Who would Miss Lin give the part to? Finally, Miss Lin came out and told Jackie that the role of Juliet was **(11)** her's. Jackie gave Kim and **(12)** I a big hug. The first thing Jackie said was, "I owe it all to my friends, **(13)** who believed in me!"

1. _____

2. _____

3. _____

4. _____

5. _____

6. _____

7. _____

8. _____

9. _____

10. _____

11. _____

12. _____

13. _____

Copyright © Perfection Learning® All rights reserved.

Grade 9 • Chapter 21: Using Pronouns **137**

CHAPTER 22 Singular and Plural Subjects

[22A] A **verb** must agree with its subject in **number**.

[22A.3] A singular subject takes a singular verb, and a plural subject takes a plural verb.

[22B.3] A verb must agree in number with an indefinite pronoun used as a subject.

EXERCISE Indicate whether the subject in each sentence is singular or plural.

_____ 1. Nobody knows the answer to the sixteenth question.
  A singular
  B plural

_____ 2. Both make new friends very easily.
  A singular
  B plural

_____ 3. None of the light bulbs have burned out yet.
  A singular
  B plural

_____ 4. Most of the flour was used to make bread.
  A singular
  B plural

_____ 5. Everyone in the three science classes takes the same test.
  A singular
  B plural

_____ 6. Several of the medals were awarded to juniors.
  A singular
  B plural

_____ 7. Most of the animals in the zoo eat at one o'clock.
  A singular
  B plural

_____ 8. None of the rain has leaked through the roof.
  A singular
  B plural

_____ 9. Neither of the twins is coming with us to the beach.
  A singular
  B plural

_____ 10. All of the new houses on Brattle Street have been sold.
  A singular
  B plural

_____ 11. A bat is in the barn.
  A singular
  B plural

_____ 12. Pigeons live on our roof.
  A singular
  B plural

_____ 13. The Joneses are feeding the cows.
  A singular
  B plural

_____ 14. The hay has been stored for winter.
  A singular
  B plural

_____ 15. Pigs definitely like to eat.
  A singular
  B plural

_____ 16. A sheep does not moo.
  A singular
  B plural

CHAPTER 22 Singular and Plural Subjects

EXERCISE Circle the verb that agrees in number with the subject.

1. He (know / knows) very little about animals.

2. I (has / have) always lived in the city.

3. A herd of goats (is approaching / are approaching) now.

4. The goats in front (is bleating / are bleating).

5. A group of pigs (is standing / are standing) there.

6. A young hog (is known / are known) as a pig.

7. Hogs in a sty (is / are) not dirty animals.

8. Hogs often (use / uses) mud to keep cool.

9. Hogs as a group (eat / eats) almost anything.

10. A hog eating scraps (is / are) quite content.

11. A farmer with hogs (feed / feeds) them well.

12. Hogs, despite their reputation, rarely (overeat / overeats).

13. Pigs at birth (weigh / weighs) less than three pounds.

14. Grown hogs (weigh / weighs) about 500 pounds.

15. The white dress (is / are) perfect for the party.

16. Pineapples (grows / grow) in tropical countries.

CHAPTER 22 Making Subjects and Verbs Agree

EXERCISE A Choose the verb that agrees with the subject in each sentence.

_____ 1. The small child _____ toward her parents.
  A runs
  B run

_____ 2. Every day the birds _____ over our house.
  A fly
  B flies

_____ 3. Jessica and Samson _____ to finish the race.
  A is trying
  B are trying

_____ 4. Their food _____ early for the dinner.
  A has been prepared
  B have been prepared

_____ 5. The cattle owned by Mr. May _____ beneath the elm trees.
  A is resting
  B are resting

_____ 6. That deer _____ through the woods at very high speeds.
  A runs
  B run

_____ 7. You _____ to get an A on the test, don't you?
  A want
  B wants

_____ 8. Unfortunately I _____ a terrible grade.
  A has received
  B have received

EXERCISE B Circle the verb that agrees with the subject in each sentence.

9. The young girl with the white gloves (is trying / are trying) to call her mother.

10. Whitney (is / are) a very serious person.

11. The chopsticks that Mary gave you (is / are) very beautiful.

12. The fortune cookies that we ate after the meal (was / were) chocolate.

13. Our cats, despite their funny names, (is / are) both very solemn animals.

14. Mr. McKenzie often (tries / try) to bowl 300.

15. Alison's best friend, Arthur, (is / are) never home when she calls.

16. Thousands of people in this city (has / have) ferrets as pets.

CHAPTER 22 Agreement and Interrupting Words

[22A.7] The agreement of a verb with its subject is not changed by any interrupting words.

EXERCISE Choose the verb that agrees with the subject in each sentence.

_____ 1. The hands of the mole _____ very much like human hands.

    A is
    B are

_____ 2. Every Sunday many people living on Pine Street _____ a baseball game.

    A organizes
    B organize

_____ 3. Flags of France, Spain, and England _____ flown over areas of Mississippi.

    A has
    B have

_____ 4. The craters of the moon _____ visible through a low-powered telescope.

    A is
    B are

_____ 5. One of Sumi's sisters _____ to Wheaton College in Illinois.

    A goes
    B go

_____ 6. The election of the Student Council officers _____ held last week.

    A was
    B were

_____ 7. A town in the Dutch West Indies _____ located in an extinct volcano.

    A is
    B are

_____ 8. Shape, as well as size, _____ determine the value of a pearl.

    A helps
    B help

_____ 9. Three people in our group _____ swimming in the ocean.

    A was
    B were

_____ 10. Ammonia, which is used in household cleaners, _____ poisonous.

    A is
    B are

_____ 11. One of the New England states _____ admitted to the Union in 1820.

    A was
    B were

_____ 12. That tree, including branches and leaves, _____ 100 tons.

    A weighs
    B weigh

_____ 13. The front tires of the abandoned car _____ worn smooth.

    A was
    B were

_____ 14. Until the nineteenth century, solid blocks of tea _____ used as money in Siberia.

    A was
    B were

_____ 15. A representative of several colleges _____ visiting our school.

    A is
    B are

_____ 16. One of the birds _____ a mockingbird.

    A is
    B are

Name _____   Date _____

CHAPTER 22 Agreement and Interrupting Words

EXERCISE Decide whether the verb agrees with the subject of the sentence. Write Y for *yes* or N for *no* in the blank. If the verb does not agree, cross it out and write the correct verb above it.

_____ 1. The lock on each of the doors are secure.

_____ 2. The cherries in this fruit smoothie is in season this month.

_____ 3. One student from among the ninth graders was elected to student council.

_____ 4. The panes of glass on this door has become smudged and dirty.

_____ 5. The book covers on all but one book is torn.

_____ 6. Huge waves from far out in the ocean is crashing to shore.

_____ 7. All of the wheels on my trusty old skateboard are now well oiled.

_____ 8. The shoes that I described to Mom was under the tree at Christmas.

_____ 9. The stories that I told the children during story hour were adventurous.

_____ 10. The letters in the mailbox in front of the house was written by Melody.

_____ 11. The final hours before the debate was spent in practice.

_____ 12. The large boxes in the lunchroom is there to collect cans for recycling.

_____ 13. Several of the emails was from Minnie.

_____ 14. Many of us who went to the library was grateful for the librarian's help.

_____ 15. The accident during the preliminary trials was disappointing to the scientist.

_____ 16. This case of apples are for Mom's cooking classes.

_____ 17. When I grew up, I realized that the monsters under my bed was only imaginary.

_____ 18. The files in the last filing cabinet, Karen, is the student records.

Name _____   Date _____

CHAPTER 22   # Compound Subjects and Indefinite Pronouns as Subjects

[22B.1] When subjects are joined by *or*, *nor*, *either/or*, or *neither/nor*, the verb agrees with the subject that is closer to it.

[22B.2] When subjects are joined by *and* or *both/and*, the verb is plural—whether the subjects are singular, plural, or a combination of singular and plural.

EXERCISEA   Choose the verb that agrees with the subject in each sentence.

_____ 1. Neither Jane nor her brothers _____ the bus.

    A rides

    B ride

_____ 2. Some raccoons and opossums _____ in cities.

    A lives

    B live

_____ 3. Either garlic or onions _____ a beef dish added flavor.

    A give

    B gives

_____ 4. The praying mantis and the ladybug _____ other bugs.

    A eat

    B eats

_____ 5. Red and white _____ the colors of the Canadian flag.

    A is

    B are

_____ 6. Both carrots and parsnips _____ root vegetables.

    A is

    B are

_____ 7. Neither the sheep nor the horses _____ wearing flea collars.

    A was

    B were

_____ 8. Both my cat and dog _____ wearing flea collars.

    A is

    B are

_____ 9. In this store every watch and clock _____ the exact time.

    A tells

    B tell

CHAPTER 22   Compound Subjects and Indefinite Pronouns as Subjects

EXERCISEB   In the following paragraph, circle the verb that agrees with the subject in each sentence.

(1) Red, yellow, and blue (is / are) the primary colors. **(2)** Dogs and certain other animals probably (does / do) not see color. **(3)** A bee or a wasp (sees / see) colors that we do not. **(4)** Neither green nor orange (is / are) a primary color. **(5)** The secondary colors, or binary colors, (is / are) produced by mixing primary colors. **(6)** Under a blue light, both red and green (looks / look) black.

(7) A background color or surrounding shades (changes / change) the appearance of a color.

(8) Yellow hues or a blue shade when placed against green (looks / look) a bit reddish. **(9)** Each tint and tone (changes / change) when mixed with a little of another shade. **(10)** Every new combination (produces / produce) its own effect.

Name _____   Date _____

CHAPTER 22 Compound Subjects and Indefinite
Pronouns as Subjects

EXERCISE Choose the verb that agrees with the compound subject.

_____ 1. The plans and arrangements for the
picnic _____ not been finalized yet.
   A has
   B have

_____ 2. Either Jennie or her brothers _____ the
Sunday newspaper.
   A delivers
   B deliver

_____ 3. Ham and cheese _____ my favorite
sandwich.
   A is
   B are

_____ 4. Every student and teacher _____
present at the special assembly.
   A was
   B were

_____ 5. Neither Mars nor Jupiter _____ as
bright as Venus.
   A is
   B are

_____ 6. Each pencil and pen _____ marked
with Karen's name.
   A was
   B were

_____ 7. Both moisture and warm air _____
needed to raise orchids.
   A is
   B are

_____ 8. Mums or carnations _____ requested
for the centerpiece on the table.
   A was
   B were

_____ 9. My softball coach and Spanish teacher
_____ Mrs. Gomez.
   A is
   B are

_____ 10. Strawberries and cream still _____ my
favorite dessert.
   A remains
   B remain

_____ 11. Red, white, and blue _____ the colors
in many flags.
   A is
   B are

_____ 12. After more than thirty years, rock-and-
roll _____ still a popular kind of music.
   A is
   B are

_____ 13. Either Pat or Cathy _____ the key to
the costume room.
   A has
   B have

_____ 14. Earthquakes and volcanoes _____
caused cities to sink beneath the sea.
   A has
   B have

_____ 15. Some tape or nails _____ needed to
hang this poster.
   A is
   B are

_____ 16. The passenger and driver of the truck
_____ not hurt in the accident.
   A was
   B were

CHAPTER 22 Using Verbs and Contractions; Natural and Inverted Order

[22B.4] The subject and the verb of an inverted sentence must agree in number.

[22C.1] The verb part of a contraction must agree in number with the subject.

EXERCISE Circle the verb form that agrees with the subject in each sentence.

1. (Has / Have) the bell rung yet?

2. (Does / Do) Marina have change for the bus?

3. (Is / Are) the man wearing glasses your uncle?

4. (Is / Are) the men in that car your cousins?

5. There (is / are) only eleven eggs in that carton.

6. On the basket (is / are) four yellow bows.

7. (Doesn't / Don't) Chester play basketball on Wednesdays?

8. Here (is / are) the list of characters in the play.

9. (Doesn't / Don't) those people have a piano?

10. (Doesn't / Don't) anyone here have the right time?

11. There (is / are) more milk in the cartons in the refrigerator.

12. (Does / Do) that book of quotations have what you're looking for?

13. At the top of the flagpole (waves / wave) the banners of both teams.

14. Here (is / are) my blue jacket with the missing buttons.

15. (Doesn't / Don't) your dog like to carry a big stick in his mouth?

16. Matilda and Larry (doesn't / don't) have the measles after all.

17. There (is / are) two truckloads of yogurt being delivered now.

18. (Doesn't / Don't) your brother Sam sell personal computers?

Name _____   Date _____

CHAPTER 22 Other Agreement Problems

[22C] Some contractions, collective nouns, and other issues can present agreement problems.

[22C.1] The verb part of a contraction must agree in number with the subject.

[22C.2] Use a singular verb with a collective noun subject that is thought of as a unit. Use a plural verb with a collective noun subject that is thought of as individuals.

[22C.3] A subject that expresses an amount, a measurement, a weight, or a time is usually considered singular and takes a singular verb.

[22C.4] Use a singular verb with certain subjects that are plural in form but singular in meaning.

[22C.5] A verb agrees with the subject of a sentence, not with the predicate nominative.

[22C.6] A title takes a singular verb.

EXERCISE A Choose the form of the verb that agrees with the subject.

_____ 1. _____ you want to join the softball team?
  A Doesn't
  B Don't

_____ 2. _____ they joining us for dinner?
  A Isn't
  B Aren't

_____ 3. That _____ sound like a normal jet engine.
  A doesn't
  B don't

_____ 4. Chihuahuas usually _____ like other Chihuahuas.
  A doesn't
  B don't

_____ 5. _____ they told about the meeting?
  A Wasn't
  B Weren't

_____ 6. _____ plants give off oxygen?
  A Don't
  B Doesn't

EXERCISE B Write the form of the verb "to be" that agrees with the subject.

_____ 7. Those singers _____ a big hit now.

_____ 8. My pottery class _____ learning about glazes.

_____ 9. *Thirteen Days* _____ a book by Robert Kennedy.

_____ 10. Computers _____ a great learning tool.

_____ 11. Eight miles of the River Seine _____ inside the city of Paris.

_____ 12. Economics _____ the subject I enjoy most this year.

_____ 13. Nearly three fourths of the earth's surface _____ covered by salt water.

_____ 14. One result of inflation _____ higher interest rates.

_____ 15. The Cardsharps _____ painted about 1590.

CHAPTER 22 Other Agreement Problems

EXERCISE Decide whether the verb agrees with the subject of the sentence. Write Y for *yes* or N for *no* in the blank. If the verb does not agree, cross it out and write the correct verb above it.

_____ 1. Don't these baby turtles look cute?

_____ 2. The orchestra are tuning their instruments.

_____ 3. Two-thirds of the questions have been answered.

_____ 4. Civics are one of her favorite college classes.

_____ 5. All of these desserts is my creation.

_____ 6. The mumps are infecting some of the children at Sarah's preschool.

_____ 7. The gang of friends is spending the day at Morty's house.

_____ 8. Doesn't all of the stars seem bright tonight?

_____ 9. Ninety days are too long to go without rain.

_____ 10. The class are taking its place in the auditorium.

_____ 11. Melinda doesn't know the rules well.

_____ 12. Michael's pants is torn at the knee.

_____ 13. Model airplanes are my hobby.

_____ 14. Is two teaspoons of salt too much for the bread dough?

_____ 15. *Field of Dreams* is one of Dad's favorite movies.

CHAPTER 22 Subject and Verb Agreement Review

EXERCISE In the paragraph below, some of the underlined verbs are incorrect. Write the correct form of the verb on the lines below. If the verb is correct, write C on the line.

The Jefferson High Theatre Troupe **(1)** <u>are mounting</u> a production of *The Pirates of Penzance* for the spring musical. *Pirates* **(2)** <u>were</u> written by the famous 19th-century duo Gilbert and Sullivan, and this production **(3)** <u>is being directed</u> by Tom Sherwood. "There **(4)** <u>is</u> a lot of great songs in this show," Sherwood said. "But the most famous and the most difficult **(5)** <u>are</u> 'The Major-General's Song.'" The words of this song **(6)** <u>is</u> hard to learn, and they **(7)** <u>are</u> sung very rapidly. The lucky actor who gets to perform the song **(8)** <u>is</u> junior Steve Nguyen. "But every actor and actress **(9)** <u>have</u> challenging songs," Sherwood added. "With Gilbert and Sullivan, all of the music **(10)** <u>demand</u> your best. Luckily, our cast **(11)** <u>is</u> up to the task." Two dollars **(12)** <u>buy</u> you a chance to find out if Sherwood is right.

1. _____

2. _____

3. _____

4. _____

5. _____

6. _____

7. _____

8. _____

9. _____

10. _____

11. _____

12. _____

CHAPTER 23 · Determining the Degree of Comparison

[23A] **Adjectives** and **adverbs** are modifiers. Most modifiers show degrees of comparison by changing form.

[23A.1] The **positivedegree** is the basic form of an adjective or an adverb. It is used when no comparison is being made.

[23A.2] The **comparativedegree** is used when two people, things, or actions are being compared.

[23A.3] The **superlativedegree** is used when more than two people, things, or actions are being compared.

EXERCISEA Select the answer that contains the correct comparative and superlative forms of each adjective or adverb.

_____ 1. warm
    A warmer, warmest
    B more warm, most warm

_____ 2. fast
    A faster, fastest
    B more fast, most fast

_____ 3. often
    A oftener, oftenest
    B more often, most often

_____ 4. hot
    A hotter, hottest
    B more hot, most hot

_____ 5. famous
    A famouser, famousest
    B more famous, most famous

_____ 6. frequently
    A frequentlier, frequentliest
    B more frequent, most frequent

_____ 7. bad
    A badder, baddest
    B worse, worst

_____ 8. good
    A better, best
    B gooder, goodest

EXERCISEB Choose the correct form of the modifier to complete each sentence.

_____ 9. The _____ twin is Roberta.
    A thin
    B thinner
    C thinnest

_____ 10. Norman Rockwell was one of America's _____ illustrators.
    A known
    B better known
    C best known

_____ 11. Colleen is the _____ of the two Compton sisters.
    A young
    B younger
    C youngest

_____ 12. Of the three finalists, Greg has the _____ chance to win.
    A little
    B less
    C least

continued

Chapter 23: Determining the Degree of Comparison *continued*

_____ 13. Rita thinks spring is the _____ season of all.

    A beautiful

    B more beautiful

    C most beautiful

_____ 14. Of all the mountains in the Andes, which is the _____?

    A high

    B higher

    C highest

_____ 15. Tony can mow the lawn _____ than his brother.

    A fast

    B faster

    C fastest

_____ 16. Which way is _____, bus or subway?

    A quick

    B quicker

    C quickest

Name _____ Date _____

EXERCISE Write the correct form of the modifier in parentheses to fill the blank in each sentence.

_____ 1. The city of London has the _____ subway system in the world. (old)

_____ 2. Which of these two pencils has the _____ point? (sharp)

_____ 3. My heart beat _____ at the audition than at the performance. (rapid)

_____ 4. Which of you two has washed the dishes _____ this week? (often)

_____ 5. To me the painting of the city is the _____ of the four. (beautiful)

_____ 6. One seagull in the flock appeared to dive _____ than the rest. (graceful)

_____ 7. Mr. Greenberg is undoubtedly the _____ person I have ever met. (kind)

_____ 8. I'm confident that I will do _____ this year than last year. (well)

_____ 9. Being close to the accident was the _____ experience of my life. (bad)

_____ 10. Barbara has even _____ time to practice than I do. (little)

_____ 11. That freight train is not the _____ one I have ever seen. (long)

_____ 12. Of the three books, which one is _____? (good)

CHAPTER 23   Determining the Degree of Comparison

EXERCISE Circle the form of the modifier that would correctly complete each sentence.

1. Today is a (sunnier/more sunnier/sunniest) day than yesterday.

2. This is a(n) (educational/more educational/educationaler) seminar.

3. My little brother always grabs the (bigger/biggest/most biggest) cookie of the batch.

4. Traffic outside my window is (noisy/noisier/more noisier) now than it used to be.

5. Pavel's school uniform is (fadeder/more faded/most faded) than anyone else's.

6. At the buffet table, I chose the (littlest sugary/less sugary/least sugary) dessert there.

7. Diana is one of the (friendlier/friendliest/most friendliest) people I know.

8. We chose the (shadier/more shadier/shadiest) picnic spot of the two.

9. My toy poodle eats (daintily/more daintily/most daintily) than your German shepherd.

10. Of all our backpacks, yours is the (heavier/more heavier/heaviest).

11. Sending an email is (quicker/more quicker/quickest) than mailing a letter.

12. Carmen is the (recentest/more recent/most recent) addition to our club.

13. I'll carry the (less heavy/less heavier/least heaviest) box of the two.

14. History class seems (long/longer/more longer) than usual today.

15. The yearbook staff is having one of their (frequent/more frequent/most frequent) work-a-thons.

16. Of the cardinal, the blue jay, and the finch, the finch is (smaller/more smaller/smallest).

17. What day has been the (happy/happier/happiest) day of your life so far?

18. Washing dishes is my (less favorite/least favorite/least favoritest) chore to do.

19. This year's drama production was (livelier/more livelier/most lively) than last year's.

20. Where is the (near/more nearer/nearest) exit?

CHAPTER 23 — Correcting Mistakes in Comparison; Avoiding Double Negatives

[23B] When you compare people or things, avoid **double comparisons, illogical comparisons**, and **comparing a thing with itself**.

[23B.1] Do not use both *-er* and *more* to form the comparative degree, or both *-est* and *most* to form the superlative degree.

[23B.2] Compare only items of a similar kind.

[23B.3] Add *other* and *else* when comparing a member of a group with the rest of the group.

[23C] It is important to know whether a word is an adjective or an adverb in order to form the comparisons correctly.

[23C.1] *Good* is always used as an adjective. *Well* is usually used as an adverb. However, when *well* means "in good health" or "attractive," it is an adjective.

[23C.2] *Bad* is an adjective and often follows a linking verb. *Badly* is used as an adverb.

[23C.3] Avoid using a **double negative.**

EXERCISE Choose the correct form of the underlined comparison. If the underlined comparison is already correct, choose *No error.*

_____ 1. Diagrams help make directions and explanations more clearer to a reader.

    A clearer
    B most clearest
    C No error

_____ 2. She was so sleepy she couldn't hardly stay awake.

    A couldn't barely
    B could hardly
    C No error

_____ 3. The sperm whale has a heavier brain than any animal.

    A than any other animal
    B than all animals
    C No error

_____ 4. More turkeys are raised in California than in any state in the United States.

    A than in all states
    B than in any other
    C No error

_____ 5. Uncle Al can hardly wait to see the Colts play again.

    A can't hardly
    B can't barely
    C No error

_____ 6. Pam hasn't done nothing about getting us tickets.

    A has done nothing
    B ain't done nothing
    C No error

_____ 7. Frank's science experiment has turned out good.

    A well
    B gooder
    C No error

_____ 8. You are the most happiest person I have ever known.

    A happier
    B happiest
    C No error

CHAPTER 23 Correcting Mistakes in Comparison; Avoiding Double Negatives

EXERCISE Rewrite each sentence to correct mistakes in comparison.

1. Elise expects to be more thinner after all that exercise.

   _____

2. The Sahara is the most largest desert in the world.

   _____

3. Elliot usually hits the ball farther than anyone on the baseball team.

   _____

4. The most earliest wristwatches were made in the 1790s.

   _____

5. That atlas appears to be the most biggest book in the library.

   _____

6. Our new car rides more smoothly than any car we've ever had.

   _____

7. After rehearsing her song, Fran sounds much more better.

   _____

8. The Russian Federation is bigger than any country in the world.

   _____

9. When Tommy's cold got worser, my mother took him to the doctor.

   _____

10. Our next-door neighbors are noisier than anyone on our street.

   _____

CHAPTER 23   Using Adjectives and Adverbs Review

EXERCISE In the paragraph below, some of the underlined modifiers are incorrect. Write the correct form of the modifier on the lines below. If the modifier is correct, write C on the line.

Margot Fonteyn was considered by many to be the **(1)** <u>finer</u> ballerina in the world. She joined the Royal Ballet after being trained by some of the **(2)** <u>famousest</u> teachers of the time. She gained her **(3)** <u>most greatest</u> fame when she began dancing with Rudolf Nureyev, a **(4)** <u>widely</u> admired Russian dancer. Together, Fonteyn and Nureyev became **(5)** <u>most</u> acclaimed than **(6)** <u>any</u> dance partners. They had a **(7)** <u>closer</u> friendship offstage, as well. When Fonteyn was diagnosed with cancer, Nureyev paid **(8)** <u>more</u> of her medical bills. Fonteyn had **(9)** <u>little</u> savings because her husband, a Panamanian diplomat, was shot and injured **(10)** <u>bad</u>. To pay his medical bills, Fonteyn continued to dance until she was 60. On her retirement, the Royal Ballet named Fonteyn its prima ballerina assoluta, an honor it hasn't bestowed on **(11)** <u>no</u> other dancer. To this day, Fonteyn's dedication and talent are greater than almost **(12)** <u>any other</u> dancer's.

1. _____

2. _____

3. _____

4. _____

5. _____

6. _____

7. _____

8. _____

9. _____

10. _____

11. _____

12. _____

CHAPTER 24 First Words and the Pronoun *I*

[24A] A capital letter signals the beginning of a new idea, whether it is in the form of a sentence, a line of poetry, or a formal outline.

[24A.1] Capitalize the first word of a sentence and of a line of poetry.

[24A.2] Capitalize the first word in the greeting of a letter and the first word in the closing of a letter.

[24A.3] Capitalize the first word of each item in an outline and the letters that begin major subsections of the outline.

[24A.4] Capitalize the pronoun *I*, both alone and in contractions.

EXERCISE Underline the fi rst letter of the word that should be capitalized.

1. what did you name your dog?

2. with one blow of his ax, Paul Bunyan toppled an oak.

3. what did Carol say at the history conference?

4. "exult O shores, and ring O bells!" (Walt Whitman)

5. i went to the play, but oh, how boring it was!

6. did Sean Connery star in six movies about James Bond?

7. If I find the book, i'll call you.

8. between 1890 and 1895, George W. Vanderbilt II had a 280-room house built for himself.

9. with only $28,000, Henry Ford began his motor company in 1903.

10. my mother named her cats Charlie and Esther.

11. "But i with mournful tread, / Walk the deck my Captain lies." (Walt Whitman)

12. Where is my English book? it was here a moment ago.

13. did you buy the Einstein calendar for next year?

14. She wrote in the poem, "after the battle was over / And the sun had gone down."

15. I'm going to the dance. are you?

CHAPTER 24   First Words and the Pronoun *I*

EXERCISE Decide whether each item is capitalized correctly.

_____ 1. when you come to the sleepover, bring a sleeping bag.

   A yes
   B no

_____ 2. I can't believe i'm going to Paris!

   A yes
   B no

_____ 3. My poem begins, "the crashing of my heart when you walk near."

   A yes
   B no

_____ 4. Why are you home this early? Is something wrong?

   A yes
   B no

_____ 5. this has been a terrific field trip, don't you think?

   A yes
   B no

_____ 6. I promise that i'll be home by curfew.

   A yes
   B no

_____ 7. where is the dress that i ironed last night?

   A yes
   B no

_____ 8. The floodwaters rose in the blink of an eye, and the townspeople raised a terrified cry.

   A yes
   B no

_____ 9. We'll be at the mall until seven o'clock.

   A yes
   B no

_____ 10. i don't see a single empty chair in this lunchroom.

   A yes
   B no

_____ 11. did you promise to pick up Janey, or did i?

   A yes
   B no

_____ 12. Where is my umbrella? do you remember where I put it?

   A yes
   B no

_____ 13. I don't eat chicken because i'm a vegetarian.

   A yes
   B no

_____ 14. Volleyball tryouts are at four o'clock in the gym.

   A yes
   B no

_____ 15. Here is a list of friends i invited to my birthday party.

   A yes
   B no

_____ 16. How did you do on the math test, Tammy?

   A yes
   B no

_____ 17. you have become quite a talented photographer.

   A yes
   B no

_____ 18. well, that was my idea. what is yours?

   A yes
   B no

CHAPTER 24 Capitalization of Proper Nouns

[24B] Capitalize proper nouns and their abbreviations.

[24B.1] Names of persons and animals should be capitalized. Also capitalize initials that stand for people's names.

[24B.2] Geographical names, which include particular places and bodies of water and their abbreviations, initials, and acronyms, are capitalized.

[24B.3] Capitalize historically important nouns, which include the names of historical events, periods, and documents and their associated initials and acronyms.

[24B.4] Names of groups, such as organizations, businesses, institutions, government bodies, teams, and political parties, should be capitalized.

[24B.5] Specific time periods and events, including the days of the week, the months of the year, civil and religious holidays, and special events, should be capitalized.

[24B.6] Names of nationalities, races, and languages should be capitalized.

[24B.7] Religions, religious holidays, and religious references, such as the names referring to the Deity, the Bible, and divisions of the Bible, should be capitalized. Also, capitalize pronouns that refer to the Deity.

[24B.8] Names of stars, planets, and constellations are capitalized.

[24B.9] Other proper nouns—such as the names of aircraft, awards, brand names, and buildings—should also begin with capital letters.

EXERCISE Choose the proper noun that should be capitalized in each group.

_____ 1. **A** dog
     B pet
     C parker
     D pooch

_____ 2. **A** person
     B one woman
     C lady
     D mary jones

_____ 3. **A** bob
     B boy
     C his son
     D his father

_____ 4. **A** boulevard
     B street
     C road
     D third avenue

_____ 5. **A** lake erie
     B river
     C the ocean
     D stream

_____ 6. **A** that city
     B a state
     C kansas city
     D a country

_____ 7. **A** mountain
     B hilltop
     C rocky mountains
     D volcano

_____ 8. **A** battle
     B world war I
     C last war
     D skirmish

continued

Chapter 24: Capitalization of Proper Nouns *continued*

_____ 9. **A** kent high school
       B college
       C school
       D university

_____ 10. **A** republican
       B party
       C political party
       D convention

_____ 11. **A** today
       B labor day
       C holiday
       D someday

_____ 12. **A** winter
       B this month
       C season
       D january

CHAPTER 24 Capitalization of Proper Nouns

EXERCISE Choose the word or words in each sentence that should be capitalized.

_____ 1. Like venus, jupiter has a thick cloud cover.
- **A** venus
- **B** cloud
- **C** jupiter
- **D** venus, jupiter

_____ 2. Twenty-one million americans now play the piano.
- **A** million
- **B** americans
- **C** million, americans
- **D** piano

_____ 3. The greatest concentration of catholics in the united states is in rhode island.
- **A** catholics
- **B** united states
- **C** rhode island
- **D** catholics, united states, rhode island

_____ 4. Is exodus the second book in the old testament?
- **A** old
- **B** exodus
- **C** exodus, old testament
- **D** testament

_____ 5. In 1976, *viking I* landed on mars.
- **A** landed
- **B** *viking*, mars
- **C** *viking*
- **D** mars

_____ 6. After the thirty years' war, the french, not the germans, became the leading watchmakers.
- **A** thirty years' war, french, germans
- **B** thirty years' war
- **C** french, germans
- **D** war

_____ 7. At night, north can be determined almost exactly by locating the position of polaris, the north star.
- **A** polaris
- **B** north star
- **C** north
- **D** polaris, north star

_____ 8. My uncle, wayne mosely, has joined the local chapter of the southwest veterinarian society.
- **A** wayne mosely
- **B** southwest
- **C** veterinarian society
- **D** wayne mosely, southwest veterinarian society

_____ 9. The diameter, density, and gravity of venus are similar to those of earth.
- **A** venus, earth
- **B** venus
- **C** earth
- **D** diameter, density, gravity

_____ 10. The lincoln memorial in washington, d.c., is the work of daniel chester french.
- **A** washington, d.c.
- **B** daniel chester french
- **C** lincoln memorial, washington, d.c., daniel chester french
- **D** lincoln memorial

_____ 11. Was william sherman a general in the american revolution or the Civil War?
- **A** general
- **B** william sherman
- **C** american revolution
- **D** william sherman, american revolution

_____ 12. Someone in the new england historical association will know who wrote the declaration of independence.
- **A** declaration
- **B** historical association
- **C** new england historical association, declaration, independence
- **D** declaration, independence

CHAPTER 24 Capitalization of Proper Nouns

EXERCISEUnderline the fi rst letter of each word that should be capitalized in the sentences below.

1. On Sunday, November 17, Tony will go whale watching aboard the schooner *seafair*.

2. On Monday, November 18, Tony plans to audition for a role on the television series *the Hospital*.

3. Tony will meet Samantha at the airport on Tuesday, November 19, to fly over the sahara.

4. On Wednesday, november 20, Tony will be doing absolutely nothing.

5. Tony travels to Des Moines, Iowa, on Thursday, November 21, to compete in the World Frisbee tournament.

6. On Friday, November 22, Tony will photograph the statues in the Roosevelt memorial for *Arts* magazine.

7. Tony will travel to Estes park, Colorado, on Saturday, November 23, to hike in the Rocky mountains.

8. On Monday, November 24, Tony will drive to Denver to do volunteer work for the american Red Cross.

9. Tony will rejoin Samantha on Tuesday, November 26, on the shores of the Great Salt lake in Utah.

10. On Wednesday, November 26, Tony will climb to the top of the Eiffel tower in Paris.

CHAPTER 24 Recognizing Proper Nouns

EXERCISEA Choose the proper noun that should be capitalized in each group.

_____ 1. **A** new england
      B my brother
      C high school
      D their parrot

_____ 2. **A** history
      B ace road
      C town
      D avenue

_____ 3. **A** bureau of taxes
      B star
      C club
      D grocery store

_____ 4. **A** author
      B bread
      C state
      D thanksgiving day

_____ 5. **A** river
      B fair
      C boston marathon
      D autumn

_____ 6. **A** goods
      B milky way
      C universe
      D shoe

_____ 7. **A** russian
      B cashmere
      C money
      D line

_____ 8. **A** paper
      B math
      C pencil
      D science 2

_____ 9. **A** sister
      B stephanie
      C jeans
      D watch

_____ 10. **A** spring
      B april
      C yard
      D water

EXERCISEB Write *YES* if the item is capitalized correctly or *NO* if it is not.

_____ 11. typing and spanish

_____ 12. the Los Angeles department of sanitation

_____ 13. the New Testament

_____ 14. nine lives cat food

_____ 15. God and his kingdom

_____ 16. the Vietnam Memorial

_____ 17. advanced geometry II

_____ 18. the American library association

_____ 19. judaism

_____ 20. *Spirit of St. Louis*

CHAPTER 24 Recognizing Proper Nouns

EXERCISE Decide whether each item is capitalized correctly. If so, write Y for *yes* in the blank. If the item is not capitalized correctly, write N for *no* in the blank. Then underline the first letter of each word that should be capitalized.

_____ 1. the sun and mars

_____ 2. Polish and Russian

_____ 3. a Presbyterian

_____ 4. the *hindenberg*

_____ 5. Cook County

_____ 6. the statue of liberty

_____ 7. a methodist

_____ 8. the War of 1812

_____ 9. the empire state building

_____ 10. Sirius and other stars

_____ 11. Fifty-Third Avenue

_____ 12. Toronto, a city in canada

_____ 13. a canadian

_____ 14. Montana

_____ 15. the Microsoft corporation

_____ 16. the Pulitzer Prize

_____ 17. sisters of mercy hospital

_____ 18. cheezco cheese

_____ 19. a college named Wellesley

_____ 20. sri lanka and japan

CHAPTER 24   Proper Adjectives

[24C] Capitalize most proper adjectives.

EXERCISEA   Decide whether each item is capitalized correctly. Write Y for *yes* or N for *no* in the blank.

_____ 1. a Jamaican cruise

_____ 2. a georgian accent

_____ 3. Italian food

_____ 4. a beach vacation

_____ 5. a British ship

_____ 6. a vietnamese pen pal

_____ 7. swiss chocolate

_____ 8. french class

_____ 9. the Victorian house

_____ 10. a porcelain plate

EXERCISEB   Rewrite each item as a proper adjective and a noun.

11. blue jeans made in France

_____

12. watches made in Switzerland

_____

13. cranberries from Cape Cod

_____

14. a movie from Britain

_____

15. cooking in the style of the South

_____

continued

Chapter 24: Proper Adjectives *continued*

16. the language of Korea

_____

17. food from India

_____

18. potatoes from Idaho

_____

19. a hockey team from Canada

_____

20. the government of Poland

_____

CHAPTER 24   Proper Adjectives

EXERCISE Decide whether each item is capitalized correctly. Write Y for *yes* or N for *no* in the blank. Then underline the first letter of each word that should be capitalized.

_____ 1. mississippi waterfront property

_____ 2. Colombian coffee

_____ 3. a european airline

_____ 4. the high school debate team

_____ 5. an English rugby team

_____ 6. the clinton era

_____ 7. southwestern pottery

_____ 8. a Shakespearean sonnet

_____ 9. a Midwestern college

_____ 10. the Californian coast

_____ 11. a labrador retriever

_____ 12. japanese sushi

_____ 13. a movie in the Hitchcock style

_____ 14. a business lunch

_____ 15. a german shepherd

CHAPTER 24 Capitalizing Correctly

EXERCISE Underline the fi rst letter of the word or words that should be capitalized in each sentence.

1. The sting of the portuguese man-of-war, a jellyfish found on this beach, is very painful.

2. My neighbors have a norwegian elkhound, which I think is a very strange name for a dog.

3. The flowers of the japanese iris can be as large as a dinner plate.

4. For dinner our hostess prepared succulent maine lobster.

5. Belinda had the lead soprano role in the operetta *patience*.

6. Did you read the ad about the sale at foot's shoe store?

7. The visitors from europe listened to a long speech by mayor margalis.

8. Was the song "greensleeves" written by an elizabethan poet?

9. The sculptures of frederic remington are often copied, especially *bronco buster*.

10. One houseplant that grows easily in a temperate climate is the african violet.

CHAPTER 24 Capitalizing Titles

[24D] Capitalize certain titles.

[24D.1] Capitalize a title showing office, rank, or profession when it comes directly before a person's name.

[24D.2] Capitalize a title that is used alone when the title is being substituted for a person's name in direct address.

[24D.3] Capitalize a title showing a family relationship when it comes directly before a person's name. When the title is used as a name, or when the title is substituted for a person's name in direct address, it is also capitalized.

[24D.4] Capitalize the first word, the last word, and all important words in the titles of books, newspapers, periodicals, stories, poems, movies, plays, musical compositions, and other words of art.

EXERCISE A In each sentence, correct the word or words that are incorrectly capitalized (either capitalized when they should be lowercase, or lowercase when they should be capitalized). If a word should not be capitalized, draw a slash through the first letter. If a word should be capitalized, underline the first letter.

---

1. My cousin interviewed the Senator for the school paper.

2. Yes, mother, I wrote to Uncle Herbert yesterday.

3. The patients in the Doctor's office are reading magazines.

4. The song "Sunrise, Sunset" is from the show *Fiddler On the Roof*.

5. Is Professor Harris discussing the book *Moby-dick* today?

6. Ellen's aunt Dorothy saw the opera *The Magic Flute* yesterday.

7. Does Governor Evans read *Concerning the law* regularly?

8. One of the world's greatest paintings is *the Last Supper*.

EXERCISE B Choose the correct answer in each pair.

_____ 9. **A** "A worn Path"
  B "A Worn Path"

_____ 10. **A** *The Empire Strikes Back*
  B *The Empire strikes Back*

_____ 11. **A** *A Tale of Two Cities*
  B *A Tale Of Two Cities*

_____ 12. **A** "The Garden Party"
  B "The garden party"

_____ 13. **A** *The Sound Of Music*
  B *The Sound of Music*

_____ 14. **A** "I've Been Working On The Railroad"
  B "I've Been Working on the Railroad"

Name _____   Date _____

CHAPTER 24   Capitalizing Titles

EXERCISE Rewrite each sentence to correct the capitalization. If the sentence is already capitalized correctly, write *No error*.

1. My uncle and aunt are coming to visit mom and me.

   _____

2. The president of the United States and queen Elizabeth of England met for the first time recently.

   _____

3. My aunt Ruth is going to marry senator Tobin on Valentine's Day.

   _____

4. Thanks, sis, for helping me serve food at dr. phelps's party.

   _____

5. My brother Jeff is running for president of the Foreign Language Club.

   _____

6. The senators from our state will visit our school next Wednesday.

   _____

7. Could I stand in for the assistant coach while he is out sick, coach?

   _____

8. When did you decide to become a dentist, mr. Mosera?

   _____

9. Do you know who is the superintendent of your school district?

   _____

10. The pastor of our church knows ambassador Lang and her husband.

    _____

11. My sister is a reporter for the *washington post*.

    _____

Name

Date

CHAPTER 24 Capital Letters Review

EXERCISE In the essay below, some of the words have not been capitalized. For each word that should be capitalized, underline the first letter.

Popular music is one of the most revealing aspects of a time and place. If you want to learn about life in twentieth and twenty-first century america, one way is to look at a list of songs that have won the Academy award. each song comes from a successful movie released in a given year. In 1939, for instance, the winner was "Over the rainbow" from *the Wizard of Oz*. By contrast, the 2002 winner was "Lose Yourself" by eminem, and in 2008, the winning song was "Jai Ho," a hindi song from *Slumdog Millionaire.*

From just these three songs, we can make some observations. In "Over the Rainbow," we hear the voice of hope in the depths of the Great depression. That "Lose Yourself" won the oscar shows the growing acceptance of hip-hop in american society. The success of "Jai Ho," despite not being in english, reflects the way barriers between cultures are falling in the age of the internet. Other recent winners, such as "i Need to Wake Up," highlight growing social concerns.

There has been criticism of the Best Original song awards. The academy of motion picture arts and sciences is sometimes called uninspired or old-fashioned in its tastes. If so, perhaps its focus on what is broadly palatable makes the award even more effective as a sign of the times.

Copyright © Perfection Learning® All rights reserved.

Grade 9 • Chapter 24: Capital Letters **171**

CHAPTER 25 Classifying Sentences and Using End Marks

[25A] A sentence may be **declarative, imperative, interrogative,** or **exclamatory**.

[25A.1] A **declarative sentence** makes a statement or expresses an opinion and ends with a period.

[25A.2] An **imperative sentence** gives a direction, makes a request, or gives a command. It ends with either a period or an exclamation point.

[25A.3] An **interrogative sentence** asks a question and ends with a question mark.

[25A.4] An **exclamatory sentence** expresses strong feeling or emotion and ends with an exclamation point.

EXERCISE Label each sentence as declarative, imperative, interrogative, or exclamatory.

_____ 1. I asked for orange juice, bacon, and eggs

_____ 2. That is my favorite breakfast

_____ 3. Do you prefer pancakes or waffles

_____ 4. Please pass the butter

_____ 5. Look out, that plate is hot

_____ 6. We often have a late breakfast on Saturdays

_____ 7. Will you join us for breakfast one day soon

_____ 8. This restaurant deserves its good reputation

_____ 9. Nothing beats home cooking, though, does it

_____ 10. Hurry, or we'll miss our train

_____ 11. How far north do palm trees grow

_____ 12. I just won $10,000

_____ 13. Everyone please follow me

_____ 14. After you mow the lawn, rake up the clippings

_____ 15. Reno, Nevada, is farther west than Los Angeles

_____ 16. Which planet is closest to Earth

_____ 17. Only rarely do whooping cranes breed in captivity

_____ 18. Mother asked why you didn't empty the rubbish can

_____ 19. Go to bed right this minute

_____ 20. Two professional sports many people watch regularly are baseball and basketball

---

CHAPTER 25 Classifying Sentences and Using End Marks

EXERCISE Write the correct end mark for each sentence.

1. I asked for orange juice, bacon, and eggs _____

2. That is my favorite breakfast _____

3. Do you prefer pancakes or waffles _____

4. Please pass the butter _____

5. Look out, that plate is hot _____

6. We often have a late breakfast on Saturdays _____

7. Will you join us for breakfast one day soon _____

8. This restaurant deserves its good reputation _____

9. Nothing beats home cooking, though, does it _____

10. Hurry, or we'll miss our train _____

11. How far north do palm trees grow _____

12. I just won ten thousand dollars _____

13. Everyone please follow me _____

14. After you mow the lawn, rake up the clippings _____

15. Reno, Nevada, is farther west than Los Angeles _____

16. Which planet is closest to Earth _____

17. Only rarely do whooping cranes breed in captivity _____

18. Mother asked why you didn't empty the rubbish can___

19. Go to bed right this minute _____

20. Two professional sports many people watch regularly are baseball and basketball _____

CHAPTER 25 Other Uses of Periods

[25A.5] A period may be used in places other than at the ends of sentences.

EXERCISE Choose the correct abbreviation for each item.

_____ 1. Highway 191
    A Highw. 191
    B Hwy. 191
    C H.W. 191

_____ 2. 304 West Elm Street
    A 304 W. Elm St.
    B 304 Wst. Elm Strt.
    C 304 W. E. St.

_____ 3. General Colin Powell
    A G. Colin Powell
    B Gen. Colin Powell
    C Gener. Colin Powell

_____ 4. *anno Domini*
    A An.Dom.
    B a.D.
    C A.D.

_____ 5. United Nations
    A U.N.
    B UN
    C U. Nations

_____ 6. United States of America
    A U.S.A.
    B U. St. Amer.
    C U. S. of A.

_____ 7. Henry Wadsworth Longfellow
    A Henry W. Longfellow
    B Hen. W. Longfellow
    C Henry W. L.

_____ 8. Mister Morton
    A M. Morton
    B Mis. Morton
    C Mr. Morton

_____ 9. *post meridiem*
    A P.M.
    B pst. m.
    C *post m.*

_____ 10. Association
    A Ass'n.
    B Asn.
    C Assoc.

_____ 11. Computer Works, Incorporated
    A Computer Works, Inc'd.
    B Computer Works, Inc.
    C Computer Works, Incor.

_____ 12. ounce
    A oz
    B oc
    C oze.

_____ 13. Bachelor of Science
    A B.S.
    B Bach.S.
    C B.Sci.

_____ 14. video cassette recorder
    A v.c.r.
    B V.C.R.
    C VCR

_____ 15. teaspoon
    A tea.
    B tsp
    C tspn.

_____ 16. Wednesday
    A Wed.
    B Wed'day.
    C Wend.

_____ 17. February
    A Febr.
    B Feb.
    C Febu.

_____ 18. South Carolina
    A SC
    B S. Carol.
    C Sth. Car.

CHAPTER 25 Other Uses of Periods

[25A.5] A period may be used in places other than at the ends of sentences.

> **EXERCISE** Periods are used after the numbers and letters that are used as divisions in outlines. Add periods to the following outline.

1.	I	The way of life in the North
2.	A	Had a diversified economy
3.	1	Had farms and industry
4.	2	Had a variety of crops
5.	B	Had industry
6.	1	Had mills and factories
7.	2	Competed with Britain
8.	II	The way of life in the South
9.	A	Depended on a few cash crops
10.	B	Depended on trade with Europe

CHAPTER 25 Using Commas in a Series

[25B] Commas are used to prevent confusion and to keep items from running into one another.
[25B.1] Use commas to separate items in a series.

EXERCISE Add commas to each sentence where necessary.

---

1. December January and February are the coldest months in New England.

2. The colors of the streamers were red pink and white.

3. Are you walking biking or driving to the grocery store?

4. Today Marcia has science math history chorus and Spanish.

5. The ball rolled over the curb into the street and under a car.

6. Carl Vernick plays the trumpet draws cartoons writes poetry and repairs cars.

7. No one has told me who is coming when they are arriving or what they are bringing.

8. Does Paula's dress really have red and gold stripes a green belt and two violet ruffles?

9. The menu offered a choice of chicken and rice spaghetti and meatballs or macaroni and cheese.

10. The newspaper article told where the accident occurred why it happened and who was involved.

CHAPTER 25 Using Commas in a Series; Using Commas That Separate

[25B.2] A comma is sometimes needed to separate two adjectives that precede a noun and are not joined by a conjunction.

> **EXERCISE** Choose the word or words that should be followed by a comma. If no comma is needed, choose *No error*.

_____ 1. The longest-known sentence ever written contains 823 words 93 commas 51 semicolons and 4 dashes.

    A words, commas, semicolons, dashes
    B words, commas, semicolons
    C written, words, commas, semicolons
    D No error

_____ 2. Zip is the biggest strongest dog on the block.

    A biggest
    B biggest, strongest
    C dog
    D No error

_____ 3. Among the strangest names of towns in the United States are Accident Soso Helper and Battiest.

    A Accident, Helper
    B Accident, Soso
    C Accident, Soso, Helper
    D No error

_____ 4. Could you tell me when the library opens where it is and how I can get there?

    A me, opens, is
    B is
    C opens, is
    D No error

_____ 5. Some cacti produce beautiful delicate flowers.

    A produce, beautiful, delicate
    B beautiful
    C beautiful, delicate
    D No error

_____ 6. Mr. Roberts is the tall dignified man in the blue suit.

    A tall, dignified
    B tall
    C tall, dignified, blue
    D No error

_____ 7. The *H* in *4H Club* stands for "head heart hands and health."

    A head, heart, hands, health
    B head, heart
    C head, heart, hands
    D No error

_____ 8. My mother just bought a musical Swiss clock.

    A musical
    B musical, Swiss
    C Swiss
    D No error

_____ 9. My uncle's house is surrounded by small green shrubs.

    A green
    B small
    C small, green
    D No error

_____ 10. We store tools in a sturdy wooden box.

    A sturdy, wooden
    B sturdy
    C wooden
    D No error

continued

_____ 11. Tadpoles develop hind legs first grow front legs next and finally lose their tails.

    A first, next

    B first

    C next

    D No error

_____ 12. My father couldn't read the torn wet newspaper.

    A wet

    B torn, wet

    C torn

    D No error

_____ 13. Two Adamses two Harrisons and two Roosevelts have been president.

    A Adamses

    B Harrisons

    C Adamses, Harrisons

    D No error

_____ 14. The loud piercing alarm awakened us.

    A loud

    B loud, piercing

    C loud, piercing, alarm

    D No error

CHAPTER 25 Checking Comma Usage

EXERCISE Underline the word or words that should be followed by a comma.

1. What weighs nothing can be seen with the naked eye and makes a bag weigh less?

2. The people who answered correctly were Anna Jerome and Kai.

3. Here is a slightly more challenging longer puzzle to be solved.

4. Two fathers and two sons went fishing on a warm sunny summer day.

5. Each person caught one fish but only three fish were caught in all.

6. If there were two fathers and two sons why were only three fish caught?

7. The Pattersons and the Smiths were tired but they still went on the trip.

8. The fishermen were a grandfather a father and a son.

9. A dog a cat a gerbil and a fish were the four pets Georgia bought.

10. How can you eat read the paper and sing at the same time?

11. In the afternoon we played volleyball sipped lemonade and slapped at mosquitoes.

CHAPTER 25 Using Commas with Compound Sentences

[25B.3] Use a comma to separate the independent clauses of a compound sentence if the clauses are joined by a conjunction.

EXERCISEAdd a comma where appropriate to each sentence.

---

1. It seems early to think about next year's classes but it's always a good idea to plan ahead.

2. I need another science credit so I will take biology.

3. Biology interests me for it deals with living things.

4. I would like to sing in the chorus but I am nervous about auditioning.

5. Math is one of my favorite subjects for it is useful.

6. Are you going to take algebra and do you think I should?

7. The Shakespeare class sounds interesting but only seniors may take it.

8. I could take composition or I could take Mr. Grant's new course, Modern Fiction 1.

9. I plan to join the French Club and I want to try out for the volleyball team.

10. Playing a sport in the fall will be impossible for I will be in the marching band.

11. I am playing the French horn this year in orchestra and the trumpet in marching band.

12. I like the trumpet and French horn equally.

13. My sister used to play French horn and her friend Marla once played oboe.

14. My friend Eric and I are starting a band and our band's name is Kayak.

15. I sing and Eric writes songs.

16. We also both play guitar but now we are looking for a drummer.

17. We need a drummer and we also need a keyboard player.

18. Eric's father has a synthesizer and his uncle has an old battered piano.

19. We would like to ask Linda to join the band but she is too temperamental.

20. Eric fears that Linda would quit the band and we would be left without a keyboardist.

CHAPTER 25 Commas with Introductory Elements; Commonly Used Commas

[25B.4] Use a comma after certain introductory elements.

[25B.5] Use commas to separate the elements in dates and addresses.

[25B.6] Use a comma after the salutation of a friendly letter and after the closing of all letters.

EXERCISE Decide whether each sentence is punctuated correctly.

_____ 1. Above a glider soared gracefully.

    A yes

    B no

_____ 2. Write to Curtis Circulation Company 645 Madison Avenue, New York NY 10014 for information.

    A yes

    B no

_____ 3. Address the envelope to Patricia Hartman Ph.D., and include extra postage.

    A yes

    B no

_____ 4. Deciding the trail was too steep, the hikers turned back after two hours.

    A yes

    B no

_____ 5. After practice in the gym we will meet in room 3B.

    A yes

    B no

_____ 6. No announcement was made prior to the meeting.

    A yes

    B no

_____ 7. In 1776 54 delegates signed the Declaration of Independence in Philadelphia.

    A yes

    B no

_____ 8. After dinner I will meet you at the library.

    A yes

    B no

_____ 9. Down the chimney of our house dropped a bird's nest.

    A yes

    B no

_____ 10. Dear Uncle Nathan I will be arriving for my visit on Friday.

    A yes

    B no

_____ 11. After he was deaf, Ludwig van Beethoven still wrote music.

    A yes

    B no

_____ 12. Well water often tastes better than tap water.

    A yes

    B no

_____ 13. Waving to Mary Sue entered the bus.

    A yes

    B no

_____ 14. Insulated by thick layers of blubber whales can dive deep into the icy depths of the ocean.

    A yes

    B no

_____ 15. Into the pool jumped Randy and his friends.

    A yes

    B no

Name _____   Date _____

CHAPTER 25 **Commas with Introductory Elements; Commonly Used Commas**

> **EXERCISE** Add a comma or commas to each sentence where appropriate.

1. On July 4 1826 John Adams and Thomas Jefferson died.

2. Send the check to Rob Matthews Jr. 365 Jade Street, Springfield, IL 62702.

3. On May 30 1896 the first automobile accident in the United States occurred in New York New York.

4. On July 4, 1956 over one inch of rain fell in one minute at Unionville Maryland.

5. I signed the letter, "Sincerely Vicki Blevins."

6. Mail your requests to Ms. Lois Burbank 59 Chatham Street Greenville SC 29609.

7. On December 16 1773, the American colonists staged the famous Boston Tea Party.

8. Dear Leta
   I am glad we have become pen pals.

9. On April 30, 1812 Louisiana was admitted to the Union.

10. Write to me at P.O. Box 284 Toms River NJ 08754.

11. Yes that is a wonderful idea!

12. Well I'm not sure that I want to go there.

13. Dear Mom
    Camp has been fun so far.

14. Before the final exam I studied all my old tests.

15. Best wishes
    Simon Porter

16. While cooking vegetables lose some of their vitamins.

17. Sure I'll help you wash the car.

18. Working in the toy store after school Larry enjoyed his afternoons.

19. Signalling to Jack Roy entered the court.

20. Now this is the plan we will follow.

CHAPTER 25   **Using Commas with Direct Address and Parenthetical Expressions**

[25C] Commas are used to enclose words that interrupt the main idea of a sentence.

[25C.1] Use commas to enclose **nounsofdirectaddress** .

[25C.2] Use commas to enclose, or set off, **parentheticalexpressions** .

[25C.3] Contrastingexpressions , which usually begin with the word *not*, are also considered parenthetical expressions and should be set off by commas.

EXERCISEAdd a comma or commas to each sentence where appropriate.

---

1. Dad are you going to the game tonight?

2. I just don't understand the second math problem Jenny.

3. On the other hand the first problem was easy.

4. Peru and Venezuela for example are countries in South America.

5. To tell the truth I don't want to go to Jim's party.

6. Hurry Hannah before it starts to rain.

7. Texas produces more oil than any other state of course.

8. In fact the electronic flash was invented in 1931.

9. Color film moreover was introduced in 1935.

10. Generally speaking my camera takes good photographs Jeff.

CHAPTER 25 Using Commas with Direct Address and Parenthetical Expressions

EXERCISE Choose the word or words, if any, that should be followed by a comma for each sentence.

_____ 1. Do you like riddles my friend?
  A Do, you
  B like, riddles
  C riddles
  D No commas

_____ 2. Generally speaking I do.
  A Generally
  B speaking
  C speaking, I
  D No commas

_____ 3. For example what kind of milk is preferred by the invisible man?
  A example
  B example, preferred
  C preferred
  D example, kind, milk

_____ 4. The answer to that of course is evaporated milk.
  A that
  B that, course
  C course
  D that, course, is

_____ 5. Here Richard is another one.
  A Here
  B Richard
  C Here, Richard
  D No commas

_____ 6. What word in your opinion contains all 26 letters?
  A What
  B word
  C opinion
  D word, opinion

_____ 7. The answer is *dictionary* according to the riddle expert.
  A is
  B is, *dictionary*
  C *dictionary*
  D riddle

_____ 8. Monique it's your turn now I think.
  A Monique
  B turn
  C now
  D Monique, now

_____ 9. Why to the scientist's surprise did the bacterium cross the microscope?
  A Why
  B Why, scientist's
  C Why, surprise
  D Why, bacterium

_____ 10. The answer obviously is to get to the other slide.
  A answer, obviously
  B answer
  C obviously
  D No commas

CHAPTER 25 Using Commas with Direct Address and Parenthetical Expressions

> **EXERCISE** Add a comma or commas to each sentence where appropriate.

1. What's for dinner tonight Mom?

2. A fly's taste buds surprisingly enough are in its feet.

3. Ladies and gentlemen please be seated.

4. Ostriches for instance have wings but cannot fly.

5. I already gave Dave the grocery list including the dog food.

6. Yes Thomas you may work with Toni.

7. I had a wonderful time by the way with my friend.

8. My weight because I have been exercising is down a bit.

9. The movie after all won an award.

10. Could you tell me please if Dr. Saltus is in?

11. Jefferson was the third president not the second.

12. Of course Margaret you can join us.

13. The witch-hazel plant blooms only in winter I think.

14. I'll give you the list Tim at Saturday's meeting.

15. Nina like her two brothers is good at math.

16. The book in my opinion was the best I ever read.

17. Perhaps the next bus which arrives in 20 minutes will be less crowded.

18. On the other hand palm trees live up to 100 years.

CHAPTER 25 Commas with Appositives

[25C.4] Use commas to enclose most **appositives** and their modifiers.

EXERCISEChoose the word or words that should be followed by a comma. If no comma is needed, choose *No error*.

_____ 1. Antarctica a large mass of land wasn't really explored until the twentieth century.

    A Antarctica, land
    B Antarctica
    C No error

_____ 2. The name *Caroline* means "strong."

    A name
    B name, *Caroline*
    C No error

_____ 3. Carmel one of the oldest towns in California was founded as a Spanish mission.

    A Carmel
    B Carmel, California
    C No error

_____ 4. Have you and Joanie ever visited Columbia the capital of South Carolina?

    A Columbia
    B Columbia, capital
    C No error

_____ 5. Zachary Taylor the twelfth president never voted in his life.

    A Taylor
    B Taylor, president
    C No error

_____ 6. Francisco Coronado a Spanish explorer brought the first horse to the Americas in 1540.

    A Coronado, explorer
    B Francisco, Spanish
    C No error

_____ 7. The novelist Rudyard Kipling wrote *Kim*.

    A novelist, Kipling
    B novelist
    C No error

_____ 8. Hindi the official language of India is spoken by only 35 percent of the population.

    A Hindi
    B Hindi, India
    C No error

_____ 9. Alvin Parker once flew a glider a plane without a motor 644 miles.

    A plane, motor
    B glider, motor
    C No error

_____ 10. I just bought a new pocket-size thesaurus a most useful reference book.

    A thesaurus
    B new, thesaurus
    C No error

_____ 11. Streck Avenue a street on the east side of the city is closed for construction.

    A Avenue
    B Avenue, city
    C No error

_____ 12. The British writer Sir Arthur Conan Doyle wrote the Sherlock Holmes stories.

    A writer
    B writer, Doyle
    C No error

_____ 13. My best friend Nancy sits beside me in most classes.

    A friend, Nancy
    B Nancy
    C No error

_____ 14. That paint color sea foam green will look good on the bathroom walls.

    A paint, green
    B color, green
    C No error

CHAPTER 25 Commas with Appositives

EXERCISE Add a comma or commas to each sentence where appropriate.

1. My first pet a brown hamster provided me much joy.

2. One common abbreviation *etc.* is a shortened form of the words *et cetera.*

3. My pet adoption agency Pet Rescue needs volunteer foster families.

4. Your favorite vegetable cabbage is on sale at the market.

5. The scientist carefully studied photographs of "the red planet" Mars.

6. Texas the largest state in the continental United States borders Mexico.

7. The largest state in the United States Alaska borders Canada.

8. Does my name James Buchanan mean anything to you?

9. NATO the North Atlantic Treaty Organization was formed in 1950.

10. The Prairie Dogs our team are playing the Panthers.

11. The Historical Society held its meeting in the oldest building in town City Hall.

12. My birthday, February 14 falls on Valentine's Day.

13. The actress Alicia Silverstone starred in *Clueless* a modern retelling of *Emma* by Jane Austen.

14. The late afternoon sun will come from that direction west.

15. Our band director Mr. Moore told us about an excellent band camp.

CHAPTER 25   Writing with Nonessential and Essential Elements

[25C.5] Use commas to set off **nonrestrictiveparticip ialphrasesandclauses** .

[25C.6] If a participial phrase or a clause is **restrictive**—essential to the meaning of a sentence, no commas are used.

EXERCISEChoose the word or words, if any, that should be followed by a comma for each sentence.

_____ 1. *Salmagundi* an amusing word names a mixture of chopped meats anchovies or pickled herrings onions lemon juice and oil.

    A *Salmagundi*, meats, herrings, onions, juice

    B *Salmagundi*, meats, anchovies, herrings, onions, juice

    C *Salmagundi*, word, meats, herrings, onions, juice

    D *Salmagundi*, word, meats, anchovies, herrings, onions, juice

_____ 2. Delighted by the word Washington Irving named his humorous periodical *Salmagundi*.

    A word

    B word, Irving

    C word, periodical

    D word, Irving, periodical

_____ 3. The title was used again by a magazine that appeared in the 1960s.

    A title

    B magazine

    C title, appeared

    D No commas

_____ 4. The cheese called Gorgonzola also has an interesting name.

    A cheese, Gorgonzola

    B cheese

    C Gorgonzola

    D No commas

_____ 5. This cheese originally came from the Italian village of Gorgonzola which is located near the city of Milan.

    A cheese, Gorgonzola

    B cheese

    C Gorgonzola

    D No commas

_____ 6. The stag alarmed by the loud and sudden noise raised its magnificent head.

    A stag, loud

    B stag, noise

    C noise, magnificent

    D No commas

_____ 7. People who work on high bridges and buildings must have nerves of steel.

    A People, bridges

    B bridges, buildings

    C People, buildings

    D No commas

_____ 8. A flock of wild geese all flying in a V-shaped formation passed high above us.

    A geese, formation

    B flock, geese, formation

    C formation

    D No commas

CHAPTER 25 Writing with Nonessential and Essential Elements

EXERCISE Decide whether each sentence contains an essential element (choice A) or whether it should be rewritten using commas (shown in choice B).

_____ 1. I just bought in-line skates my new workout equipment.

   A essential
   B I just bought in-line skates, my new workout equipment.

_____ 2. We saw two bear cubs hiding in a hollow tree.

   A essential
   B We saw two bear cubs, hiding in a hollow tree.

_____ 3. The pronghorn antelope living only in North America has no close relatives.

   A essential
   B The pronghorn antelope, living only in North America, has no close relatives.

_____ 4. A sport that many Scots enjoy is curling.

   A essential
   B A sport, that many Scots enjoy, is curling.

_____ 5. Curling which resembles bowling is played on ice.

   A essential
   B Curling, which resembles bowling, is played on ice.

_____ 6. Huskies warmed by their thick coats are able to sleep in the snow.

   A essential
   B Huskies, warmed by their thick coats, are able to sleep in the snow.

_____ 7. Ogunquit which is on the ocean is a resort town in southeastern Maine.

   A essential
   B Ogunquit, which is on the ocean, is a resort town in southeastern Maine.

_____ 8. Where is the quartz watch that Dad gave you for your birthday?

   A essential
   B Where is the quartz watch, that Dad gave you for your birthday?

_____ 9. Mount McKinley located near the Arctic Circle may well be the world's coldest mountain.

   A essential
   B Mount McKinley, located near the Arctic Circle, may well be the world's coldest mountain.

_____ 10. An English novel that I really enjoyed reading is _David Copperfield_.

   A essential
   B An English novel, that I really enjoyed reading, is _David Copperfield_.

_____ 11. Samuel Houston for whom the city of Houston was named was a frontier hero.

   A essential
   B Samuel Houston, for whom the city of Houston was named, was a frontier hero.

_____ 12. Wolfgang Amadeus Mozart gave a concert at an age when most children are just starting school.

   A essential
   B Wolfgang Amadeus Mozart gave a concert at an age, when most children are just starting school.

CHAPTER 25 Writing with Nonessential and Essential Elements

EXERCISE Rewrite each sentence using commas. If the sentence is written correctly, write *No error.*

1. The man who is pictured on the $10,000 bill is Salmon P. Chase.

   _____

2. Arthur's uncle wants to buy a fishing pole that is made of fiberglass.

   _____

3. The Sandwich Islands which are now called the Hawaiian Islands were discovered by Captain Cook.

   _____

4. An inch of rain covering one city block weighs about 160 tons.

   _____

5. This is the tulip that won first prize at the flower show yesterday.

   _____

6. The poisonous Portuguese man-of-war has tentacles that may trail as long as 40 feet.

   _____

7. This cuckoo clock made in Germany is a present for our grandparents' anniversary.

   _____

8. The other morning we saw Patty who was waiting for the Munsey Street bus.

   _____

9. Playing cards were issued as money to French soldiers stationed in Canada in the seventeenth century.

   _____

10. The heaviest organ in the human body is the liver which weighs an average of three-and-a-half pounds.

    _____

11. Buckingham Palace which is the home of England's royal family has been the royal residence since 1837.

    _____

CHAPTER 25 End Marks and Commas Review

> **EXERCISE**No end marks or commas have been included in the paragraph below. Insert the correct punctuation marks where they belong.

John Green is a writer of novels for young adults He lives in Indianapolis Indiana but he grew up in Alabama His first novel *Looking for Alaska* was published in 2005 and won the prestigious Michael L Printz Award from the American Library Association His other works include *An Abundance of Katherines* the short story "Freak the Geek" and *Paper Towns* which he is adapting as a screenplay On January 1 2007 Green and his brother Hank began a year-long series of daily video blogs short video diaries posted online called Brotherhood 2.0 John's clever comments and Hank's silly catchy songs inspired a following of thousands of self-proclaimed "nerdfighters" Following the Brotherhood project the Green brothers continued their online presence at nerdfighters.com

CHAPTER 26 Using Italics (Underlining)

[26A] Italics are printed letters that slant to the right. Italics are used for long titles, foreign words, and words or numbers used as words. When you are writing by hand, underline words that should be in italics.

[26A.1] Italicize (underline) letters, numbers, and words when they are used to represent themselves. Also italicize (underline) foreign words that are not generally used in the English language.

[26A.2] Italicize (underline) the titles of long written or musical works that are published as a single unit. Also italicize (underline) the titles of periodicals, movies, radio and television series, paintings and sculptures, and the names of vehicles. All words in the title should be italicized.

EXERCISE Choose the answer that correctly uses italics in each sentence.

_____ 1. All five vowels appear in the word education.

    A All five vowels appear in the word *education.*

    B All five vowels appear in the *word* education.

_____ 2. The words heart and earth have exactly the same letters.

    A The *words* heart and earth have exactly the same *letters.*

    B The words *heart* and *earth* have exactly the same letters.

_____ 3. A reporter from the Newton News attended the meeting.

    A A reporter from the *Newton News* attended the meeting.

    B A reporter from the *Newton* News attended the meeting.

_____ 4. The ocean liner Olympus is sailing to France.

    A The ocean liner *Olympus* is sailing to France.

    B The ocean liner Olympus is sailing to *France.*

_____ 5. M*A*S*H was one of TV's longest running series.

    A *M*A*S*H* was one of TV's longest running series.

    B M*A*S*H was one of *TV's* longest running series.

_____ 6. Did you ever see the movie Black Beauty?

    A Did you ever see the *movie* Black Beauty?

    B Did you ever see the movie *Black Beauty*?

_____ 7. Black Beauty was originally a book by Anna Sewell.

    A Black Beauty was originally a *book* by Anna Sewell.

    B *Black Beauty* was originally a book by Anna Sewell.

_____ 8. Smash hit is an expression that comes from baseball.

    A *Smash hit* is an expression that comes from baseball.

    B Smash hit is an expression that comes from *baseball.*

_____ 9. Emily now has a subscription to Seventeen.

    A Emily now has a *subscription* to Seventeen.

    B Emily now has a subscription to *Seventeen.*

_____ 10. As You Like It is one of the plays the Old Globe will perform this season.

    A *As You Like It* is one of the plays the Old Globe will perform this season.

    B As You Like It is one of the plays the *Old Globe* will perform this season.

Name _____   Date _____

CHAPTER 26 Using Italics (Underlining)

EXERCISE Write *YES* if the sentence correctly uses italics or *NO* if it does not.

_____ 1. *Facetious* contains the vowels *a, e, i, o,* and *u.*

_____ 2. *Watts Towers* is a group of sculptures in Los Angeles.

_____ 3. Who is the *hero* in Casablanca?

_____ 4. Do you listen to Car Talk on the *radio*?

_____ 5. We're taking a train ride on the *Canyon Express.*

_____ 6. Why do phone numbers in movies always begin with *three* 5s?

_____ 7. Jerold checked *the TV Guide* for the evening's listings.

_____ 8. How many *yes*'s were counted during the vote?

_____ 9. What did you think of the movie *The Grapes of Wrath*?

_____ 10. Turn to the photograph of *the sculpture The Dream.*

_____ 11. After reading National *Velvet,* I wanted a horse of my own.

_____ 12. My brother and I enjoy watching reruns of *Law and Order.*

_____ 13. The Dictionary of National Biography is abbreviated *DNB.*

_____ 14. Look at this interesting *article* in Newsweek on schools.

_____ 15. Tryouts for *Our Town* will be held in the drama teacher's classroom.

_____ 16. Try not to use too *many* verys in your writing.

_____ 17. May I borrow your copy of *the Washington Post*?

CHAPTER 26 Using Italics (Underlining)

EXERCISE In each sentence, underline the words or phrases that should be italicized.

1. The expression going full blast began in the steel mills.

2. Before preparing his speech, Pete bought a copy of the book 10,000 Jokes, Toasts, and Stories.

3. The word committee has two m's, two t's, and two e's.

4. Who sang the tenor's part in The Marriage of Figaro?

5. The Boston Globe recently ran an article on nutrition.

6. What does vincit omnia veritas mean?

7. I hope to fly on the Concorde someday.

8. In around 1500, Bosch painted The Ship of Fools.

9. The Pirates of Penzance is a famous light opera.

10. Is the Daily Mirror London's largest newspaper?

11. The launching of Sputnik I began the space age.

12. Henry has just finished reading Things Fall Apart.

13. My 2's look like Q's.

14. The word bud has many meanings.

15. E pluribus unum is printed on several U.S. coins.

16. What does corazon mean in English?

Name _____ Date _____

[26B] **Quotationmarks** always come in pairs. They are placed at the beginning and at the end of certain titles and uninterrupted quotations.

[26B.1] Use quotation marks to enclose the titles of chapters, articles, stories, one-act plays, short poems, and songs. The entire title should be in quotation marks.

EXERCISEA If the sentence uses quotation marks correctly, write C on the line. If it uses quotation marks incorrectly, write I.

_____ 1. Tourism "Is Up" is the lead story in the *Miami Herald*.

_____ 2. Edgar Allan Poe wrote the short stories "The Pit and the Pendulum" and The Gold Bug.

_____ 3. I read "All Summer in a Day" in the Ray Bradbury book *A Medicine for Melancholy and Other Stories*.

_____ 4. Did you read the chapter "Health and Nutrition" in your science book?

_____ 5. "The Old Lady Shows Her Medals" is a one-act play, but "The Diary of Anne Frank" has two acts.

_____ 6. Who sang the song "Bridge over Troubled Water"?

_____ 7. "Glorious Jones or the Catnip Hangover" is a very humorous chapter in the book *The Fur Person*.

_____ 8. The Sea and "Sinbad's Ship" is the first part of Rimsky Korsakov's symphonic suite Scheherazade.

EXERCISEB Add quotation marks where needed in each sentence.

---

9. Two of Gwendolyn Brooks's most famous poems are We Real Cool and Kitchenette Building.

10. Did you read chapter five, Planning a Vegetarian Menu?

11. Amazing Grace is my grandmother's favorite song.

12. I used Animal Activism, an article from *Animal News*, in my report.

13. I wrote my own one-act play, All About Me.

14. Have you read Hemingway's story The Snows of Kilimanjaro?

15. No one knows who wrote Western Wind, a poem.

CHAPTER 26 Using Italics (Underlining) and Quotation Marks with Titles

EXERCISE In the following sentences, add quotation marks where needed and underline the words or phrases that should be italicized.

1. The poem called The Sharks was written by Denise Levertov.

2. The well-known children's story Hansel and Gretel comes from Germany.

3. The article Eagle's Nest in that magazine has interesting pictures.

4. Emily Dickinson wrote a lovely poem called Hope Is the Thing with Feathers.

5. The same poet describes a train in her poem I Like to See It Lap the Miles.

6. The assignment for tomorrow is to finish the fifth chapter of Jane Eyre.

7. When Kelly opens the door, we'll sing Happy Birthday.

8. Whistle While You Work was sung by the seven dwarfs in the movie Snow White.

9. One story by the Mississippi writer Eudora Welty is A Visit of Charity.

10. Jay's article for the school paper is entitled Yesterday and Tomorrow.

11. Should You Jog? is an article in Newsweek.

12. One song from the show Peter Pan is called I Won't Grow Up.

13. Mowing and Birches are poems by Robert Frost.

14. One chapter in Personal Care is called Your Teeth.

15. We sang all the stanzas of On Top of Old Smokey.

CHAPTER 26 Using Quotation Marks with Direct Quotations

[26B.2] Use quotation marks to enclose a person's exact words.

[26B.3] Begin each sentence of a direct quotation with a capital letter.

EXERCISE Choose the sentence in which quotation marks are used correctly.

_____ 1. **A** A "well-known" problem in logic begins with an angry king saying, You are only a commoner!

B A "well-known problem" in logic begins with an angry king saying, "You are only a commoner!"

C A well-known problem in logic begins with an angry king saying, "You are only a commoner!"

D A "well-known" problem in logic begins with an angry king saying, "You are only a commoner!"

_____ 2. **A** He continues, Only under one "condition" may you marry the princess.

B He continues, "Only under one condition may you marry the princess."

C "He continues," Only under one condition may you marry the princess.

D He continues, "Only under one condition may you marry" the princess.

_____ 3. **A** "I will fulfill any condition," the confident young man declares.

B "I will fulfill any condition," the confident young man "declares."

C I will fulfill any "condition," the confident young man declares.

D I will fulfill any condition, "the confident young man declares."

_____ 4. **A** "I know," agrees the princess, that you will succeed.

B "I know, agrees the princess, that you will succeed."

C "I know," agrees the princess, "that you will succeed."

D I know, agrees the princess, "that you will succeed."

_____ 5. **A** You "need only choose one of two slips of paper," the king continues.

B "You" need only choose one of two slips of paper, the king continues.

C "You need only choose" one of two slips of paper, the king "continues."

D "You need only choose one of two slips of paper," the king continues.

_____ 6. **A** On one will be written the word *"marriage,"* he explains, and on the other the words *"no marriage."*

B "On one will be written the word" *marriage,* he explains, "and on the other the words" *no marriage.*

C "On one will be written the word *marriage,*" he explains, "and on the other the words *no marriage.*"

D On one will be written the word *marriage,* "he explains," and on the other the words *no marriage.*

_____ 7. **A** Later the young man overhears the king whisper to his adviser, "I will write the words *no marriage* on both slips."

B "Later" the young man overhears the king whisper to his adviser, "I will write the words *no marriag*e on both slips."

C "Later the young man overhears," the king whisper to his adviser, "I will write the words *no marriage* on both slips."

D Later the young man overhears "the king whisper to his adviser," I will write the words *no marriage* on both slips.

CHAPTER 26 # Using Quotation Marks with Direct Quotations

EXERCISE In each sentence, add quotation marks where needed.

1. My little sister is always telling riddles, said Gail.

2. Henry asked, What has eighteen legs and catches flies?

3. It's a baseball team! declared Norman.

4. I was going to answer that, Gail stated.

5. All right, she continued, I'll ask an even sillier one.

6. She asked, What has a hundred pairs of legs but can't walk?

7. The answer must be a dead centipede, announced Norman.

8. That could be the answer, replied Gail, but it's not the one I know.

9. I think I know what has a hundred pairs of legs but can't walk, Henry said.

10. He continued, grinning, It's 100 pairs of pants.

11. Report to the field now, ordered the coach.

12. Elbert Hubbard once said, Don't make excuses—make good.

13. It is easy, observed Aesop, to be brave from a safe distance.

14. I always forget my locker combination when I'm in a rush, announced Leslie.

15. Rain is forecast for tomorrow. Maybe we should cancel the picnic, Betty suggested.

16. You all know your parts well, the drama coach told the actors. You shouldn't be nervous.

Name **_____**   Date **_____**

CHAPTER 26 Using Quotation Marks with Direct Quotations

EXERCISE Write C if the sentence is punctuated correctly or I if it is punctuated incorrectly. If a sentence is incorrect, add quotation marks where needed and cross out any quotation marks that have been placed incorrectly.

_____ 1. Sung-ki said that the kitten was wandering, lost and hungry.

_____ 2. Elena yelled, Watch out for that wasp!

_____ 3. "Honesty, he stated," is a good character trait to develop.

_____ 4. Chloe said "she would walk the dog for me."

_____ 5. Ms. Estefan announced, "This class period will be silent reading time. Use it wisely."

_____ 6. "Yikes!" Is this house haunted? screeched Marty.

_____ 7. "Which movie, Jon asked, do you want to see?"

_____ 8. Brianna said she can't resist buying the latest CDs by all her favorite artists.

_____ 9. "Tonight," I am going to dinner with my dad, said Juan Carlos.

_____ 10. Who said that this was a shortcut?

_____ 11. "I'm sorry," Ann apologized, that I forgot the DVDs.

_____ 12. Margo stated, "We all need to help. Our goal is to raise $100."

_____ 13. "Of course," said Mom, "I'm going to the open house."

_____ 14. You should never feed the bears, the park attendant warned.

Copyright © Perfection Learning® All rights reserved.   Chapter 26: Italics and Quotation Marks **199**

CHAPTER 26 Using Commas and End Marks with Quotation Marks

[26B.4] Use a comma to separate a direct quotation from a speaker tag. Place the comma inside the closing quotation marks.

[26B.5] Place a period inside the closing quotation marks when the end of the quotation comes at the end of the sentence.

[26B.6] Place a question mark or an exclamation point inside the closing quotation marks when it is part of the quotation.

[26B.7] When a question mark or exclamation mark is part of the whole sentence, it is placed *outside* the closing quotation marks.

EXERCISE Choose the answer that correctly adds commas and end marks with quotation marks for each sentence.

_____ 1. My little sister hasn't told me any new riddles lately Gail announced

    A "My little sister hasn't told me any new riddles lately" Gail announced!

    B "My little sister hasn't told me any new riddles lately," Gail announced.

_____ 2. Henry declared I have one

    A Henry declared "I have one".

    B Henry declared, "I have one."

_____ 3. He asked Why is an island like the letter *T*

    A He asked, "Why is an island like the letter *T*?"

    B He asked "Why is an island like the letter *T*?"

_____ 4. I've never heard that one said Gail

    A "I've never heard that one," said Gail.

    B "I've never heard that one", said Gail.

_____ 5. She continued I think I can guess the answer, though

    A She continued, "I think I can guess the answer, though"?

    B She continued, "I think I can guess the answer, though."

_____ 6. An island is like the letter *T* because they are both surrounded by water stated Gail confidently

    A "An island is like the letter *T* because they are both surrounded by water", stated Gail confidently.

    B "An island is like the letter *T* because they are both surrounded by water," stated Gail confidently.

continued

Chapter 26: Using Commas and End Marks with Quotation Marks *continued*

_____ 7. You guessed it declared Henry

    A "You guessed it" declared Henry!

    B "You guessed it!" declared Henry.

_____ 8. He then asked What can you place in your right hand that you cannot place in your left hand

    A He then asked, "What can you place in your right hand that you cannot place in your left hand?"

    B He then asked, "What can you place in your right hand that you cannot place in your left hand."

_____ 9. I don't know that one said Gail and I can't guess the answer, either

    A "I don't know that one," said Gail, "and I can't guess the answer, either."

    B "I don't know that one," said Gail "and I can't guess the answer, either".

_____ 10. The answer stated Henry is your left elbow

    A "The answer," stated Henry, "is your left elbow."

    B "The answer," stated Henry "is your left elbow".

CHAPTER 26 Using Commas, End Marks, and Capital Letters with Direct Quotations

EXERCISE Write C if a sentence is punctuated and capitalized correctly. Write I if it is punctuated and capitalized incorrectly.

_____ 1. "Appearances often are deceiving," writes Aesop as the moral to the fable "The Wolf in Sheep's Clothing."

_____ 2. "In another fable," he writes, "familiarity breeds contempt."

_____ 3. "Do not count your chickens," Aesop warns, "Before they are hatched."

_____ 4. "The gods help them that help themselves", advises this fable writer.

_____ 5. Do you remember the fox's comment, "I am sure the grapes are sour"?

_____ 6. "The Rats and the Cat" includes the question, "who shall bell the cat"?

_____ 7. "Come with us to the baseball game"! Eugene and Betsy urged.

_____ 8. Hale said, "My Chihuahuas each weigh only a pound."

_____ 9. "The ancient Egyptians first began to make glass in 3500 B.C." Karen explained.

_____ 10. "When is the test in English" Cindy asked?

_____ 11. "There are two sides to every argument" he said "until you take a side."

_____ 12. Quentin asked, "Did you know that the Navajos are the largest Native American tribe in America?"

_____ 13. "The traffic was terrible", Dad complained.

_____ 14. "It doesn't matter where a man comes from," Henry Ford once said. "we hire a man, not his history."

_____ 15. "I just learned," Mary said, "that a year on Jupiter is twelve times longer than a year on Earth."

_____ 16. Moy said, "Terns migrate halfway around the world twice a year."

_____ 17. "Did you know," Clyde asked "That blood is six times thicker than water?"

_____ 18. Tim suggested "you can cook the hot dogs at the picnic. I will set out chips and drinks."

CHAPTER 26 Using Commas, End Marks, and Capital Letters with Direct Quotations

EXERCISE Rewrite each sentence, adding capital letters, quotation marks, and other punctuation marks where needed.

1. Is Finland or California larger we asked

    _____

2. Someone answered the state of California is larger

    _____

3. Marvin exclaimed that greyhound was clocked at 14.17 miles an hour

    _____

4. Roy boasted I passed my driver's test today

    _____

5. The end of reading is not more books Holbrook Jackson said but more life

    _____

6. I almost fell out of my chair when Mr. Banner announced we'll skip the quiz today

    _____

7. You're taking my coat Alice warned

    _____

8. My science teacher joked if it weren't for Edison, we'd be watching TV by candlelight

    _____

9. You're picking poison ivy Mavis shouted

    _____

10. I just learned Kara stated that lightning often strikes the same spot more than once

    _____

CHAPTER 26 Italics and Quotation Marks Review

EXERCISE Read each sentence and add quotation marks, punctuation, capital letters, or underlining (for italics) as needed.

1. I can't decide, I said if Wuthering Heights or Dracula is my favorite novel.

2. Regina announced, when my sister said I do, I cried like a baby.

3. With expertise like the governor's, Todd said, it's a wonder the state isn't bankrupt.

4. Ahmad couldn't help but feel schadenfreude when his rival lost the race.

5. Douglas Adams wrote, "time is an illusion, lunchtime doubly so."

6. The more I say the word spoon, the weirder it sounds.

7. "Go, go, go" Dad urged the football team on TV.

8. If Superman has an S on his chest, why doesn't Batman have a B?

9. Laura kept a miniature version of The Thinker on her desk for inspiration.

10. Today's newspaper featured an article titled Cat Rescues Fireman from Tree.

11. There's no reason to panic, everyone, Arnold whispered from under the desk.

12. Elvis Presley's last number one song was Suspicious Minds in 1969.

13. Jessica is serving on the USS Nimitz, an aircraft carrier in the Pacific.

14. This new job at the electronics store fits me to a T, Shane declared.

15. Where are you off to today Dr. Beeks inquired.

CHAPTER 27 Singular and Plural Possessive Nouns

[27A.1] Add 's to form the possessive of a singular noun.

[27A.2] Add only an apostrophe to form the possessive of a plural noun that ends in *s*.

[27A.3] Add 's to form the possessive of a plural noun that does not end in *s*.

EXERCISE Identify whether each item is a singular or plural possessive form.

_____ 1. grape's
   A singular
   B plural
   C either

_____ 2. girls'
   A singular
   B plural
   C either

_____ 3. James's
   A singular
   B plural
   C either

_____ 4. penny's
   A singular
   B plural
   C either

_____ 5. teeth's
   A singular
   B plural
   C either

_____ 6. sons-in-law's
   A singular
   B plural
   C either

_____ 7. shelf's
   A singular
   B plural
   C either

_____ 8. boxes'
   A singular
   B plural
   C either

_____ 9. woman's
   A singular
   B plural
   C either

_____ 10. Antonio's
   A singular
   B plural
   C either

_____ 11. oil company's
   A singular
   B plural
   C either

_____ 12. mice's
   A singular
   B plural
   C either

_____ 13. sheep's
   A singular
   B plural
   C either

_____ 14. trophies'
   A singular
   B plural
   C either

CHAPTER 27 — Forming the Possessive

EXERCISE Choose the correct form of the word or words that should be possessive.

_____ 1. Are men shoe sizes different from women?

    A men's, women's
    B men's
    C women's

_____ 2. The Drama Club presentation this year was awesome.

    A Drama's
    B Club's
    C Club's, this's

_____ 3. My uncle store is a few minutes walk from here.

    A uncle's, minute's
    B uncle's
    C uncle's, minutes'

_____ 4. My brother picture appeared in Madison newspaper.

    A Madison's
    B brother's, Madison's
    C brother's

_____ 5. The girls and boys uniforms have been handed out.

    A boys'
    B girls', boys'
    C girls'

_____ 6. Sarah sisters got jobs at a children day camp.

    A Sarah's, children's
    B children's
    C Sarah's, sister's, children's

_____ 7. Jill won the National Film Association annual award.

    A Film's
    B Association's
    C Film's, Association's

_____ 8. A secretary job involves more duties than a receptionist.

    A secretary's, receptionist's
    B secretary's
    C receptionist's

_____ 9. After the ride the horses were put in Carlos barn.

    A horses'
    B Carlos's
    C horses's, Carlos's

_____ 10. My sister-in-law car is bright red.

    A sister's-in-law
    B sister-in-law's
    C sister-in-law's, car's

CHAPTER 27 Forming the Possessive

EXERCISE Write the correct possessive form for each phrase.

1. the hamster belonging to Henry

   _____

2. the platter belonging to the hostess

   _____

3. the platters belonging to the hostesses

   _____

4. the voice of her mother-in-law

   _____

5. the decision of the commander in chief

   _____

6. the dressing room for men

   _____

7. the tail that belongs to it

   _____

8. an idea of someone

   _____

9. two bicycles—one belonging to Tim and one belonging to Lily.

   _____

10. the room shared by Nate and Cooper.

    _____

11. the speech that you gave

    _____

12. a chair for anyone

    _____

13. the sale at the home of Bob and Judy

    _____

14. the newspaper from Monday

    _____

CHAPTER 27 Forming Contractions

[27A.9] Use an apostrophe in a contraction to show where one or more letters have been omitted.

EXERCISE Choose the contraction(s) that can be made within each sentence.

_____ 1. "Please do not step on the flowers," requested Ellie.

   A Please'd
   B don't
   C o'the
   D don't, o'the

_____ 2. "I know that you will do well," insisted Mrs. Garner.

   A I'ow
   B that'ou
   C that'ou, you'll
   D you'll

_____ 3. Emily urged, "Let us leave this place now."

   A Emily'rged
   B Let's
   C Let's, th'place
   D th'place

_____ 4. The detective whispered, "They are turning the corner now."

   A Th'detective
   B Th'detective, They're
   C They're
   D Th'detective, th'corner

_____ 5. "There is a bee flying around this room!" exclaimed Mario.

   A There's
   B There's, flying'round
   C flying'round
   D There's, th'room

_____ 6. The train conductor announced, "We are arriving in Belmont."

   A conductor'nounced
   B We're
   C 'n Belmont
   D We're, 'n Belmont

_____ 7. "You are absolutely and completely wrong," Michael insisted.

   A You're
   B You're, absolutely'n'completely
   C absolutely'n'completely
   D Michael'sisted

_____ 8. Mr. Yen asked, "Who is going to peel the potatoes?"

   A M'Yen
   B M'Yen, Who's
   C Who's
   D Who's, th'potatoes

_____ 9. "Can you tell whether it is raining?" asked the guide.

   A Can'ou
   B Can'ou, it's
   C it's
   D its

_____ 10. "If Dalia does not go, I will go," I insisted.

   A doesn't
   B doesn't, I'll
   C I'll
   D I'll, I'sisted

Name _____   Date _____

CHAPTER 27 Forming Contractions

EXERCISE Write the contraction correctly for each group of words.

_____ 1. there is

_____ 2. do not

_____ 3. we will

_____ 4. they are

_____ 5. are not

_____ 6. I am

_____ 7. did not

_____ 8. he would

_____ 9. who is

_____ 10. let us

_____ 11. we are

_____ 12. has not

_____ 13. they will

_____ 14. it is

_____ 15. does not

_____ 16. that is

_____ 17. will not

_____ 18. you are

_____ 19. is not

_____ 20. I would

CHAPTER 27 Semicolons

[27B.1] Use a semicolon(;) between the clauses of a compound sentence that are not joined by a conjunction.

EXERCISE Choose the answer in which a semicolon is correctly added to form a compound sentence.

_____ 1. Katie is going Marc is not.

    A Katie is going; Marc is not.

    B Katie is; going Marc is not.

_____ 2. The piano was out of tune the violin was too.

    A The piano was out of tune; the violin was too.

    B The piano was out; of tune the violin was too.

_____ 3. My brother is learning French my sister is studying Spanish.

    A My brother is learning; French my sister is studying Spanish.

    B My brother is learning French; my sister is studying Spanish.

_____ 4. A rabbit appeared the lettuce in the garden disappeared.

    A A rabbit appeared the lettuce; in the garden disappeared.

    B A rabbit appeared; the lettuce in the garden disappeared.

_____ 5. Sharon is writing to Mr. Travis now I will write later.

    A Sharon is writing to Mr. Travis now; I will write later.

    B Sharon is writing to Mr. Travis; now I will write later.

_____ 6. I had a splinter in my toe Foster removed it.

    A I had a splinter; in my toe Foster removed it.

    B I had a splinter in my toe; Foster removed it.

_____ 7. The party was a success everyone enjoyed it.

    A The party was a success; everyone enjoyed it.

    B The party was a success everyone; enjoyed it.

_____ 8. Marcos was born in this country his parents were born in Venezuela.

    A Marcos was born; in this country his parents were born in Venezuela.

    B Marcos was born in this country; his parents were born in Venezuela.

_____ 9. The clouds disappeared the sun lit up the world.

    A The clouds disappeared; the sun lit up the world.

    B The clouds disappeared the sun; lit up the world.

_____ 10. Ms. Wilson is an excellent teacher she always explains things clearly.

    A Ms. Wilson is an excellent teacher; she always explains things clearly.

    B Ms. Wilson is an excellent; teacher she always explains things clearly.

CHAPTER 27 Semicolons

[27B.2] Use a semicolon between clauses in a compound sentence that are joined by certain conjunctive adverbs or transitional words.

> **EXERCISE** Add a semicolon and comma in the correct places in each sentence.

1. We must hurry otherwise we will be late.

2. The summer has been unusually dry therefore the danger of fires has increased.

3. The cheese smelled terrible however it tasted wonderful.

4. Friday is their anniversary accordingly we should get their gift today.

5. The package looked interesting moreover it was addressed to me.

6. Seat belts are easy to use nevertheless some people don't wear them.

7. Most seat belts are quite comfortable furthermore they can save your life.

8. Don't ignore your seat belt instead wear it.

9. Dylan will be eighteen next week consequently she will be able to vote.

CHAPTER 27 Colons

[27C.1] Use a colon before most lists of items, especially when the list comes after the expression *the following*. Commas should separate items in the list.

[27C.4] Use a colon between hours and minutes, between Bible chapters and verses, and in business letters.

> **EXERCISE** If the sentence is punctuated correctly, write *YES* on the line. If it is not punctuated correctly, write *NO*.

_____ 1. Kathleen left the Boston airport at 1040 a.m. and arrived in Bermuda at 110 p.m.

_____ 2. I have relatives in: Kentucky, Utah, and Arizona.

_____ 3. While you're at the drugstore, please buy: aspirin, toothpaste, and cotton balls.

_____ 4. Grant made note of his favorite Bible verse, I Corinthians 13:13.

_____ 5. For the hike you should bring the following a snack, a canteen of water, and sunscreen.

_____ 6. The ocean floor is divided into the following three main regions: continental shelf, slope, and abyss.

_____ 7. At 1115 a.m. the minister read Psalms 62 5, the text for his sermon.

_____ 8. I've been very busy taking care of: two rabbits, one cat, three dogs, and a turtle.

_____ 9. In colonial times medicines included the following: powdered frogs, crabs' eyes, and pine bark.

_____ 10. Cargo planes carry almost anything white mice, toupees, and even small private planes.

_____ 11. Dear Sir or Madam

_____ 12. For the project you'll need these items: colored pencils, poster board, glue, and markers.

_____ 13. The meal contained: beef enchiladas, guacamole, and Spanish rice.

_____ 14. These are the names of the people in my family: Bill, Danielle, Chris, and Kate.

_____ 15. These are several kinds of trees in the schoolyard oak, maple, elm, and cottonwood.

_____ 16. The top scorers on today's quiz are: Juan, Kareem, and Taylor.

CHAPTER 27 Colons

EXERCISE Add colons where necessary. If a sentence or phrase is correct as it is, write *CORRECT* on the line.

_____ 1. My basic needs are these water, food, oxygen.

_____ 2. I'll meet you near the boat dock at 10 30 a.m.

_____ 3. Dear Senator

_____ 4. The items to put in the refrigerator are the butter, the cheese, and the fruit.

_____ 5. These were the colors in the painting red, orange, yellow, and black.

_____ 6. She began her study of the New Testament by turning to Matthew 1 1.

_____ 7. These are my favorite plays by William Shakespeare *A Midsummer Night's Dream, Hamlet,* and *Twelfth Night.*

_____ 8. The ingredients are steamed vegetables, chopped onions, spices, and egg roll wrappers.

_____ 9. Your chores for the week are the following disposing of trash, washing dishes, and walking Rex.

_____ 10. Your new curfew is 9 00 p.m. on weeknights and 10 30 p.m. on weekends.

CHAPTER 27 Hyphens

[27D.1] Use a **hyphen(-)** to divide a word at the end of a line.

EXERCISE If the hyphen correctly shows where each word could break if it needed to be divided at the end of a line, write *YES* on the line. If it does not, write *NO*.

_____ 1. kinder-garten

_____ 2. a-board

_____ 3. sil-ly

_____ 4. sur-prise

_____ 5. Thank-sgiving

_____ 6. sun-ny

_____ 7. Missis-sippi

_____ 8. curl-y

_____ 9. war-mth

_____ 10. bicy-cle

_____ 11. choc-olate

_____ 12. strawber-ries

_____ 13. John-son

_____ 14. cre-dit

_____ 15. his-tory

_____ 16. exuberant-ly

_____ 17. sneak-ing

_____ 18. conc-rete

_____ 19. ex-president

_____ 20. bro-ther-in-law

CHAPTER 27 Dashes and Parentheses

[27E] **Dashes(—)and** **parentheses()** are used like commas in some situations to separate certain words or groups of words from the rest of the sentence.

[27E.1] Use **dashes(—)** to set off an abrupt change in thought.

[27E.2] Use dashes to set off an appositive that is introduced by words such as *that is, for example,* or *for instance.*

[27E.3] Use dashes to set off a parenthetical expression or an appositive that includes commas.

[27E.4] Use **parentheses()** to enclose information that is not related closely to the meaning of the sentence.

EXERCISEChoose A for *incorrect* if the sentence should contain dashes or parentheses rather than commas. If a sentence is correct as is, choose B for *correct.*

_____ 1. Miles Davis, 1926–1991, was an influential jazz musician in America.

    A incorrect

    B correct

_____ 2. These pottery shards, see Figure 10.2, were found at the site.

    A incorrect

    B correct

_____ 3. The sky, which turned dark and stormy, discouraged us from going outside.

    A incorrect

    B correct

_____ 4. Here is a refill on your soda, sorry for that spill.

    A incorrect

    B correct

_____ 5. Dorris Lessing, who was born in 1919 in Britain, is a novelist.

    A incorrect

    B correct

_____ 6. The Sherlock Holmes stories, see list on page 162, total over 50.

    A incorrect

    B correct

_____ 7. I need the garlic press, there it is, to press the cloves of garlic.

    A incorrect

    B correct

_____ 8. The American Civil War, 1861-1865, is the subject of the novel *Across Five Aprils.*

    A incorrect

    B correct

_____ 9. The Miltons, whom I met at a party, are coming to dinner tonight.

    A incorrect

    B correct

_____ 10. When we arrive, watch where you're driving!, we'll set up the tent first.

    A incorrect

    B correct

_____ 11. The doe, a female deer, darted across the hikers' path.

    A incorrect

    B correct

_____ 12. The gorillas, about whom the documentary will be made, fascinate everyone who meets them.

    A incorrect

    B correct

_____ 13. The aforementioned authors, Edgar Allan Poe, Sir Arthur Conan Doyle, and Wilkie Collins, all wrote mystery stories.

    A incorrect

    B correct

_____ 14. Gerbils, which are small rodents, make good pets for some children.

    A incorrect

    B correct

CHAPTER 27 Dashes and Parentheses

EXERCISE Rewrite each sentence, adding either parentheses or dashes where needed.

1. The Gestapo founded in 1933 was the state secret police of Nazi Germany.

_____

2. During these years 1998 and 1999 I lived with my grandparents.

_____

3. Do you know may I ask a quick question where the car keys are?

_____

4. You may borrow these clothes those shoes also if you return them in good condition.

_____

5. The mako shark see the photograph on the next page belongs to the same family as the great white shark.

_____

6. My mom Principal Wyatt to you will be a chaperone at the party.

_____

7. Move the poster to your right there! and tack down the corners.

_____

8. The costly flood see sidebar is finally receding.

_____

CHAPTER 27 Other Punctuation Review

EXERCISE Read each sentence and add punctuation as needed.

1. Kevin has been learning the shamisen a type of Japanese instrument from his aunt.

2. We looked for the missing retainer in Roberts and Katys cars.

3. A houseplant needs three things light, water, and soil.

4. On her last report card, Shawna got As in English and Algebra.

5. Asha had seen messes before especially her own but nothing like this.

6. Grandpa likes to go on about the lines to see *Star Wars* back in 77.

7. The Big Dipper is probably the best known of the constellations.

8. The world's three tallest buildings are found in Dubai, United Arab Emirates, Shanghai, China, and Kowloon, Hong Kong.

9. This wasnt the first time Gary had come home late, but it was the first time he hadnt called first.

10. A presidential veto can be overridden by a two thirds vote of the Congress.

11. Hybrid cars reduce carbon emissions, furthermore, they lower gasoline costs.

12. In the central time zone, *The Tonight Show* starts at 10 35.

13. Several Argentinian families, including about two dozen children, live permanently in an ice cold Antarctic village called Base Esperanza.

14. Stumbling, shaken, from the roller coaster, Andre insisted he hadn't gotten his two dollars worth of thrills.

15. If there was one thing Karen dreaded, it was going to her aunt and uncles house for dinner.

CHAPTER 28 Spelling Patterns

[28A.1] When you spell words with *ie* or *ei*, *i* comes before *e* except when the letters follow *c* or when they stand for the long-a sound.

[28A.2] Words ending with a syllable that sounds like "seed" are usually spelled with -*cede*. Only one word in English is spelled with -*sede*, and only three words are spelled with -*ceed*.

> **EXERCISE** Choose the word in each group that is spelled correctly. Use a dictionary if you need help.

_____ 1. **A** fiesta
      B fieesta
      C feista

_____ 2. **A** overweieght
      B overweight
      C overwieght

_____ 3. **A** recedes
      B receedes
      C resedes

_____ 4. **A** conseding
      B conceeding
      C conceding

_____ 5. **A** superceeding
      B superseding
      C superceding

_____ 6. **A** preisthood
      B preesthood
      C priesthood

_____ 7. **A** inefficient
      B inefficent
      C inefficeint

_____ 8. **A** outfeilder
      B outfilder
      C outfielder

_____ 9. **A** reindeer
      B reiendeer
      C riendeer

_____ 10. **A** deity
      B diety
      C dieity

_____ 11. **A** disbeleif
      B disbeleef
      C disbelief

_____ 12. **A** foreign
      B foreiegn
      C foriegn

_____ 13. **A** interceed
      B intercede
      C intersede

_____ 14. **A** medeival
      B medeieval
      C medieval

_____ 15. **A** feerce
      B feirce
      C fierce

_____ 16. **A** grieving
      B greiving
      C greeving

_____ 17. **A** peirce
      B pierce
      C peerce

_____ 18. **A** proteen
      B protein
      C protien

_____ 19. **A** antesedent
      B anteceedent
      C antecedent

_____ 20. **A** conceeted
      B conceited
      C concieted

CHAPTER 28 Spelling Patterns

EXERCISE Write each word correctly on the line. If it is spelled correctly, write *CORRECT*.

_____ 1. spiceist

_____ 2. counterfit

_____ 3. exceedingly

_____ 4. twenty-ieght

_____ 5. soveriegn

_____ 6. re-interpret

_____ 7. neigh

_____ 8. dieit

_____ 9. juicyest

_____ 10. sleiegh

_____ 11. thiers

_____ 12. insufficiency

_____ 13. cheifly

_____ 14. piety

_____ 15. siezure

CHAPTER 28 Plurals

[28B] Most nouns form their plural form by adding -*s* or -*es* to the singular form. Some nouns form their plurals in other ways.

EXERCISE Choose the word in each group of three plurals that is misspelled. Use a dictionary if necessary.

_____ 1. **A** butterflies
      B snapsdragon
      C hummingbirds

_____ 2. **A** thiefs
      B clefs
      C wolves

_____ 3. **A** bookcaseses
      B dressers
      C tables

_____ 4. **A** chimneys
      B latchkeys
      C monkies

_____ 5. **A** hoaxs
      B boxes
      C axes

_____ 6. **A** dictionaries
      B theorys
      C aviaries

_____ 7. **A** cameos
      B patioes
      C volcanoes

_____ 8. **A** ellipses
      B algae
      C bacteriums

_____ 9. **A** Frenches
      B Chinese
      C British

_____ 10. **A** daughter-in-laws
      B brothers-in-law
      C fathers-in-law

_____ 11. **A** ferries
      B dairies
      C inquirys

_____ 12. **A** &s
      B $'s
      C #s

_____ 13. **A** stitches
      B lunches
      C benchs

_____ 14. **A** midwifes
      B jackknives
      C headscarves

_____ 15. **A** theses
      B crisises
      C oases

_____ 16. **A** *Us*
      B *I's*
      C *A's*

_____ 17. **A** attorneys general
      B coats of arms
      C bird of preys

_____ 18. **A** dummies
      B attornies
      C flurries

_____ 19. **A** cantoes
      B banjos
      C oboes

_____ 20. **A** bamboos
      B zoos
      C cuckooes

_____ 21. **A** insfielder
      B breadwinners
      C troublemakers

_____ 22. **A** rages
      B placeces
      C appetites

CHAPTER 28 Plurals

EXERCISE A Write the misspelled word correctly on the line preceding the group of words.

_____ 1. 1940s   50s   1980's

_____ 2. waifs   staffs   turves

_____ 3. parties   remedies   replys

_____ 4. convoys   turkies   essays

_____ 5. brides-to-be   maid-of-honors   best men

_____ 6. overpasses   crocusses   addresses

_____ 7. gassss   bosses   dresses

_____ 8. reindeers   mongooses   dormice

EXERCISE B Write the correct spelling of the plural of each word.

_____ 9. ox

_____ 10. cherry

_____ 11. torpedo

_____ 12. soprano

_____ 13. library

_____ 14. story

_____ 15. flue

_____ 16. box

_____ 17. princess

_____ 18. pulley

Name   Date

CHAPTER 28 Spelling Numbers

[28C.1] Spell out numbers that can be written in one or two words. Use numerals for other numbers. Always spell out a number that begins a sentence.

EXERCISE Choose the sentence that is written correctly.

_____ 1. **A** Ava and Jake tried to call their father 10 times, but each time they got his voicemail.
B Ava and Jake tried to call their father ten times, but each time they got his voicemail.

_____ 2. **A** If you want to catch the exhibit, you should go before the tenth of April.
B If you want to catch the exhibit, you should go before the 10th of April.

_____ 3. **A** The actor Will Smith was born in 1968.
B The actor Will Smith was born in Nineteen Sixty-Eight.

_____ 4. **A** 68 yellow ribbons have been tied to the trunk of that giant oak tree.
B Sixty-eight yellow ribbons have been tied to the trunk of that giant oak tree.

_____ 5. **A** Jorge's address is 302 West 12th Street.
B Jorge's address is 302 West Twelfth Street.

_____ 6. **A** She sold her paintings for more than one hundred thousand dollars.
B She sold her paintings for more than $100,000.

_____ 7. **A** 90 percent of our class passed the math test.
B Ninety percent of our class passed the math test.

_____ 8. **A** The Slovins have invited an eighth person to their party.
B The Slovins have invited an 8th person to their party.

_____ 9. **A** Highway One Hundred runs alongside the ocean.
B Highway 100 runs alongside the ocean.

_____ 10. **A** Lipstick was first introduced in 1915.
B Lipstick was first introduced in nineteen fifteen.

_____ 11. **A** I ate sushi for the 1st time today.
B I ate sushi for the first time today.

_____ 12. **A** Lara owns 185 baseball cards, 109 football cards, and 30 hockey cards.
B Lara owns 185 baseball cards, 109 football cards, and thirty hockey cards.

_____ 13. **A** Our algebra class will no longer be held in Room 167.
B Our algebra class will no longer be held in Room One Hundred Sixty-Seven.

_____ 14. **A** The 3 nations whose tourists spend the most money abroad are the United States, Germany, and Japan.
B The three nations whose tourists spend the most money abroad are the United States, Germany, and Japan.

Name _____   Date _____

CHAPTER 28 **Spelling Numbers**

EXERCISE Rewrite each sentence that contains numbers that are written incorrectly. Write *CORRECT* on the line for any sentences that don't need rewritten.

1. There were 5 turtles, 3 frogs, and 1 snake in the box.

   _____

2. The 2nd trip we took this summer was to Nepal.

   _____

3. There are sixty-six U.S. cities with the name Fairview.

   _____

4. The third person to cross the finish line was Suni.

   _____

5. On pages ninety through 101, you will find a short biography of the singer John Lennon.

   _____

6. 100 people have fallen ill from food poisoning this year.

   _____

7. The community play begins production on June 22.

   _____

8. 2, 4, 6, 8, and 10 are the first 5 even numbers.

   _____

9. Her first novel was published in two thousand eight.

   _____

10. Chaplin's film *Modern Times* was released in nineteen thirty-five.

    _____

CHAPTER 28 Prefixes and Suffixes

[28.D] A **prefix** is placed in front of a base word to form a new word. A **suffix** is placed after a base word to create a new word.

> **EXERCISE** Identify the choice that *incorrectly* adds a prefix or suffix to a root word. Use a dictionary if necessary.

_____ 1. **A** motivation
    B incureable
    C permitting

_____ 2. **A** vigorrous
    B perilous
    C gracious

_____ 3. **A** rexamine
    B dissolving
    C irrational

_____ 4. **A** impeachment
    B deterent
    C readiness

_____ 5. **A** intervene
    B unnoticed
    C disatisfied

_____ 6. **A** underate
    B impeach
    C disturb

_____ 7. **A** extinguish
    B override
    C ilogical

_____ 8. **A** monopolize
    B uneeded
    C biannual

_____ 9. **A** stunning
    B feellings
    C darken

_____ 10. **A** shallowness
    B losing
    C deeppen

_____ 11. **A** queasily
    B merryment
    C happiness

_____ 12. **A** redden
    B journeyed
    C apathettic

_____ 13. **A** possesion
    B ovation
    C separation

_____ 14. **A** mishap
    B adition
    C antihero

_____ 15. **A** abunddant
    B needed
    C winding

_____ 16. **A** insaneity
    B ration
    C breakable

_____ 17. **A** theatrical
    B sunniness
    C uncontrolable

_____ 18. **A** enjoyable
    B conclusion
    C lazyness

_____ 19. **A** clueless
    B slowness
    C waneing

_____ 20. **A** smilled
    B laughing
    C funniest

_____ 21. **A** foggier
    B exertion
    C oozzing

_____ 22. **A** re-organize
    B reordering
    C rehearsal

CHAPTER 28 Prefixes and Suffixes

EXERCISE Circle the words in which a prefix or suffix is incorrectly added to a root word. Then write the words correctly on the lines below.

My little brother is such a troublmaker. He's always thinking up stunts he can pull on people. He thinks it's going to increase his popularrity, but he usually ends up angry because people are avoidding him.

Yesterday, for instance, he acted nice by asking me if I wanted to share some macaroni and cheese with him after school. Even though his sincerity was questionnable, I was hungry, so I agreed. As soon as I took my first bite, my ears got red and my forehead started to sweat. I asked him angryly what he had put in the macaroni to make it so spicey. That's when he told me he had put two or three—or *twelve*—drops of tobasco sauce in it. I was seetheing, but I was so concerned with getting my mouth to cool down that my brother escaped before I could lay into him.

It's stuning to me that he's never hurt anyone with his "harmless" pranks. I do know one thing: we'll never regain the chuminess we used to have as long as he continues this zanyness. Until he starts adherring to the "Do unto others . . ." rule, he will be a giggantic pest to me.

_____   _____

_____   _____

_____   _____

_____   _____

_____   _____

Name _____ Date _____

CHAPTER 28 **Spelling Review**

> **EXERCISE** In the sentences below, some of the underlined words and phrases are spelled incorrectly. Write the correct spelling of the word(s) on the line before each sentence. If the word(s) are spelled correctly, write C on the line.

_____ 1. On the annual nature walk, students photographed <u>elks</u>, <u>deers</u>, rabbits, and squirrels.

_____ 2. China dominated the medal count in Olympic <u>diveing</u> in 2008.

_____ 3. There were eleven <u>justice of the peaces</u> at the courthouse meeting.

_____ 4. Henrietta used several <u>criterias</u> to choose the perfect new pet.

_____ 5. It is <u>illegal</u> to share most music files with your friends.

_____ 6. Jorge's soup recipe suffered from a certain <u>thiness</u>.

_____ 7. Last summer, the family toured Universal <u>Studioes</u> and saw a movie set.

_____ 8. You would be surprised how many houses have <u>mouses</u> living in them.

_____ 9. Nora's favorite part of summer was watching the <u>fireflies</u> at dusk.

_____ 10. Shanti and Benny were counting the days until August <u>twenty-fourth</u>, when the new horror movie opened.

_____ 11. Mona could <u>happyly</u> spend a day <u>re-reading</u> her old diaries.

_____ 12. Until he took the <u>reins</u>, Jack had been nervous about horseback riding.

_____ 13. Only <u>12</u> people have walked on the surface of the moon.

_____ 14. Gail likes to spend her <u>liesure</u> time listening to music from the <u>1960's</u>.

_____ 15. After tying up the boat at the dock, Martin <u>proceded</u> to hop into the water for a swim.

APPENDIX Power Rules

[Rule1] Use only one negative form for a single negative idea.

[Rule9] Use the contraction *'ve* (not of) when the correct word is *have*, or use the full word *have*. Use *supposed* instead of *suppose* and *used* instead of *use* when appropriate.

[Rule10] For sound-alikes and certain words that sound almost alike, choose the word with your intended meaning.

EXERCISE The following letter contains errors. For each underlined word or phrase, correct the error on the lines below.

Dear Editor,

In the last issue, you criticized the Franklin High Talent Show for being disorganized. As one of the participants, I must say you **(1)** haven't got no right to attack us for a few minor slipups.

Now, it's true we **(2)** should of held a rehearsal beforehand, but we **(3)** didn't have no time the week after auditions. Also, there was no way we **(4)** could of known that Corey Summerfeld would **(5)** brake his finger and go to the hospital. Jim Tanaka had to replace him even though he didn't know the **(6)** peace we were playing. When Shelly Williams asked everyone to get up onstage and dance, there **(7)** wasn't nothing we could do to stop them. Finally, it wasn't the performers' fault when the spotlight **(8)** blue out.

I **(9)** use to think this paper was fair, but if you're not going to give us **(10)** no credit for our success, then I'm not going to trust you on anything else.

Sincerely,

Jenna Mahoney

---

1. _____

2. _____

3. _____

4. _____

5. _____

6. _____

7. _____

8. _____

9. _____

10. _____

APPENDIX **Power Rules**

[Rule2] Use the mainstream past tense forms of regular and irregular verbs.

[Rule3] Use verbs that agree with the subject.

[Rule6] Use a consistent verb tense except when a change is clearly necessary.

EXERCISE The following article contains errors. For each underlined word or phrase, correct the error on the lines below.

Most video game players **(1)** <u>has heard</u> of *Pong*, a 1972 game. But did you know video games **(2)** <u>was</u> around as early as 1947? The earliest known electronic game **(3)** <u>is called</u> Cathode Ray Tube Amusement Device. It was a missile simulator based on World War II radar displays.

The year 1951 **(4)** <u>seed</u> two more games introduced. One was a chess program for an early computer. The other **(5)** <u>is</u> a machine called NIMROD that **(6)** <u>plays</u> a math game called Nim. Other simple games, such as Tic Tac Toe, **(7)** <u>was programmed</u> in the next few years.

The next breakthrough **(8)** <u>comed</u> in 1966 when the first home video game system **(9)** <u>were developed</u> (though it would not be released until 1972). In 1971, the first coin-operated video games **(10)** <u>debut</u>, a year before the famous *Pong*.

1. _____ 6. _____

2. _____ 7. _____

3. _____ 8. _____

4. _____ 9. _____

5. _____ 10. _____

APPENDIX Power Rules

[Rule4] Use subject forms of pronouns in subject position. Use object forms of pronouns in object position.

[Rule5] Use standard ways to make nouns possessive.

> **EXERCISE** The following letter contains errors. For each underlined word, correct the error on the lines below.

Dear Mr. Akwasi,

I am writing to introduce my son, Charles Horn, who will be an exchange student in your class this year. Charlie is a bright young man. **(1)** <u>Him</u> and his friends enjoy making web videos and playing their guitars. The **(2)** <u>bands'</u> sound isn't polished, but they make up for it in enthusiasm.

At school **(3)** <u>Charlies'</u> best subjects are art and photography. He's not as strong in math or science, but **(4)** <u>him</u> and **(5)** <u>me</u> have a deal. He has to finish his homework before he can go over to his **(6)** <u>friends</u> house.

There's one thing I should warn you about, though: Charlie might get pretty homesick for his sweetheart, Rose. **(7)** <u>Her</u> and Charlie have been dating for a month, and while it makes my wife and **(8)** <u>I</u> happy to see them so devoted, I know it'll break his heart, and probably **(9)** <u>Roses</u>, too, for him to be away so long.

Anyway, I'm sure you'll be happy with your **(10)** <u>classes</u> newest member. Take care of him for me.

Regards,

Richard Horn

1. _____   6. _____

2. _____   7. _____

3. _____   8. _____

4. _____   9. _____

5. _____   10. _____

APPENDIX Power Rules

[Rule7] Use sentence fragments only the way professional writers do, after the sentence they refer to and usually to emphasize a point. Fix all sentence fragments that occur before the sentence they refer to and ones that occur in the middle of a sentence.

[Rule8] Use the best conjunction and/or use punctuation for the meaning when connecting two sentences. Revise run-on sentences.

EXERCISE The following article contains sentence fragments and run-on sentences. Correct each error on the lines below.

---

(1) In 1861, two stray dogs became the unofficial mascots of San Francisco, California. (2) Bummer, a black Newfoundland, and Lazarus, a mongrel. (3) Lazarus got his name because he had been injured, Bummer nursed him back to health by bringing him scraps of food and huddling next to him for warmth. (4) Within a few days. (5) Lazarus was healthy. (6) The two dogs began begging together they also caught rats in a saloon. (7) They once reportedly caught eighty-five rats. (8) In just twenty minutes.

(9) Because the saloon was popular with newspapermen. (10) Bummer and Lazarus's adventures began appearing in several local papers. (11) Well-known cartoonist Edward Jump drew the dogs in a series of cartoons. (12) He often showed them accompanying other local characters. (13) Like the man known as "Emperor of the United States." (14) The newspaper stories made the dogs so popular. (15) When a dogcatcher took Lazarus. (16) An angry mob insisted Lazarus should be set free. (17) The city government agreed, it announced that neither Lazarus nor Bummer were subject to the law against strays. (18) The dogs' fame had saved them, they roamed free for the rest of their days.

---

1. What is the best way to revise sentence 2?

_____

_____

2. What is the best way to revise sentence 3?

_____

_____

3. Combine sentences 4 and 5.

_____

_____

4. What is the best way to revise sentence 6?

_____

_____

continued

Appendix: Power Rules *continued*

5. Combine sentences 7 and 8.

   _____

   _____

6. Combine sentences 9 and 10.

   _____

   _____

7. Combine sentences 12 and 13.

   _____

   _____

8. Combine sentences 14, 15, and 16.

   _____

   _____

9. What is the best way to revise sentence 17?

   _____

   _____

10. What is the best way to revise sentence 18?

    _____

    _____

APPENDIX   Power Rules Review

EXERCISE The following article contains errors. For each underlined word or phrase, correct the error on the lines below.

There **(1)** <u>isn't no</u> more wondrous place in the world than Uluru. **(2)** <u>This famous landmark, a large sandstone rock formation in central Australia.</u> Uluru is known for changing color as the light **(3)** <u>changed</u>, sometimes appearing gray, orange, and even red. An island mountain, Uluru **(4)** <u>rise</u> 1,142 feet above the wide, flat **(5)** <u>plane</u> around it.

In 1873, a surveyor **(6)** <u>visit</u> Uluru and named it Ayers Rock in honor of a government official. **(7)** <u>Him</u> and an Afghan camel driver became the first non-Aborigines to climb the rock. Ayers Rock remained the official name for until 1993, when a dual naming policy **(8)** <u>restores</u> the native **(9)** <u>peoples'</u> traditional name to widespread use.

Uluru is now part of a national park. Though it is more than 200 miles from the nearest large town, hundreds of thousands of people **(10)** <u>visits</u> it each year. Many people climb Uluru even though the local Anangu people hold it sacred. They ask tourists not **(11)** <u>too</u> photograph parts of Uluru because some of their members are not **(12)** <u>suppose</u> to see them.

1. _____

2. _____

3. _____

4. _____

5. _____

6. _____

7. _____

8. _____

9. _____

10. _____

11. _____

12. _____